MW00795447

# Beautiful Risks

# Beautiful Risks

## Having the Courage to Teach and Learn Creatively

Ronald A. Beghetto

ROWMAN & LITTLEFIELD
*Lanham • Boulder • New York • London*

Published by Rowman & Littlefield
An imprint of The Rowman & Littlefield Publishing Group, Inc.
4501 Forbes Boulevard, Suite 200, Lanham, Maryland 20706
www.rowman.com

6 Tinworth Street, London SE11 5AL

Distributed by NATIONAL BOOK NETWORK

Copyright © 2019 by Ronald A. Beghetto

*All rights reserved.* No part of this book may be reproduced in any form or by any
electronic or mechanical means, including information storage and retrieval systems,
without written permission from the publisher, except by a reviewer who may quote
passages in a review.

British Library Cataloguing in Publication Information Available

**Library of Congress Cataloging-in-Publication Data Available**

ISBN 978-1-4758-3472-7 (cloth : alk. paper)
ISBN 978-1-4758-3473-4 (pbk. : alk. paper)
ISBN 978-1-4758-3474-1 (electronic)

∞™ The paper used in this publication meets the minimum requirements of
American National Standard for Information Sciences—Permanence of Paper
for Printed Library Materials, ANSI/NISO Z39.48-1992.

Printed in the United States of America

This book is dedicated to you,
the beautiful risk taker,
and the positive difference you make
in the learning and lives of others.

# Contents

# Preface

This book is about doing things differently. Not just to be different, but to *make a difference*. It's about thinking and acting in different ways so as to make a creative contribution to others. Whether you're a teacher, a student, an educational leader, a parent, or a coach; you have numerous opportunities to realize new and better possibilities for teaching, learning, and life.

Doing things differently is at the heart of creativity. But doing things differently is also risky. These risks are particularly pronounced in educational settings because schools and classrooms tend not to be places where thinking and acting differently is always encouraged or rewarded. Oftentimes existing ways of doing things make the most sense.

This book is about knowing when creative action is worth the risk *and* when it is not. This includes developing the awareness, courage, and confidence to support and take risks when it is beneficial to do so. It also includes being able to recognize when certain risks should be avoided.

The key is knowing when and how to take creative action in a way that not only makes sense for the situation at hand, but also makes a positive contribution. The aim of this book is to help you and your students identify the kinds of risks that are worth taking, better anticipate and navigate potential hazards associated with those risks, and maximize the potential benefits.

Ultimately, this book is for all the beautiful risk takers who want to make a creative contribution in and outside of the classroom.

# Acknowledgments

I would like to thank all the students and educators who inspire us all by taking beautiful risks on a daily basis. I want to also thank Tom Koerner, Vice President/Publisher for Education at Rowman & Littlefield for his enthusiastic encouragement and assistance. I'd also like to thank Carlie Wall and Emily Chiarelli for all of their outstanding editorial support and everyone at Rowman & Littlefield for their work on this book. Finally, I would like to thank all my colleagues, friends, and family, especially my wife Jeralynn and daughter Olivia, who provide persistent love, inspiration, and support for all my endeavors.

*Chapter One*

# Beautiful Risks

The key to personal success is knowing how to take risks.

—J. P. Byrnes (2011)

How do you think about the role risk plays in your teaching and your students' learning? If you're like most people, you may view risks in a negative light. This makes sense, particularly because risks tend to be associated with:

- impending failure—"Sophia really struggles with reading—she's one of my most 'at-risk' students,"
- recklessness—"If he values his job, he needs to stop taking so many risks with the way he teaches Shakespeare," and
- something to be avoided—"Inviting my third period students to 'be creative' is far too risky!"

Given these negative associations, most people are risk-averse (Mumford, Blair, Dailey, Leritz, & Osburn, 2006) and fear the potentially undesirable consequences associated with risk-taking (Byrnes, 2011). Taking risks, however, is not always bad. In fact, it's necessary for creative action.

Taking risks is what moves us beyond uncertainty and toward new and meaningful thoughts and actions. When we take risks, we put possibilities into play. In this way, risk taking serves as the bridge between *what is* and *what could (or should) be*. The first step toward realizing the benefits of risks requires recognizing that not all risks are the same.

The purpose of this chapter is to clarify the difference between types of risks, introduce the concept of beautiful risks, and highlight how taking beautiful risks is necessary for moving from uncertainty to creative thought and action.

## RISKS: THE GOOD, THE BAD, AND THE BEAUTIFUL

As mentioned, some risks are worthwhile, and others should be avoided. It is also important to realize that avoiding risks can also be a problem. It really boils down to knowing when and how to take risks. As Byrnes (2011) has explained,

> Sometimes it is a good idea to take a risk . . . and sometimes it is a bad idea . . . Successful individuals take risks when it is a good idea and avoid risks when it is a bad idea. In contrast, unsuccessful individuals cannot tell the difference between appropriate and inappropriate risks. As a result, they either take too many or too few risks. (p. 146)

This way of thinking about risk-taking recognizes that because life is filled with uncertainty, we often must take risks to be successful. Given that risks have potential benefits and potential hazards (Breakwell, 2014), the key is knowing when and when not to take a particular risk. Developing this knowledge starts with understanding three types of risks: the *good*, the *bad*, and the *beautiful*.

Figure 1.1 provides an overview and examples of these different kinds of risks in the context of teaching and learning. As highlighted in figure 1.1, good risks pertain to taking action on uncertainty in cases where the perceived personal benefits outweigh the perceived costs. In teaching, good risks can come in the form of seeking feedback from colleagues or trying out new instructional tools that might make your work more efficient. In learning, good risks involve seeking assistance when needed and being willing to learn new things. In both cases the action benefits the self, but not necessarily others.

Bad risks in teaching and learning involve doing things that might have a negative impact on oneself or others. This can occur from impulsive decision making and not considering the consequences. Bad risks in teaching and learning can be overt (i.e., taking a risk in a highly public way) or subtle (i.e., taking a risk that others may not recognize or notice).

Bad risk taking can also, somewhat ironically, involve being afraid or unwilling to take a good or beautiful risk. An example in teaching would be deciding not to explore a student's unexpected and potentially insightful idea for fear that it might take the lesson or discussion off track. An example in learning would be a student not sharing a unique insight that could help solve a problem out of fear of ridicule.

|  GOOD | 👎 BAD 👎 |  |
|---|---|---|
|  | |  |

**How do I know?**
The potential **personal benefits** outweigh the potential personal costs.

**Teacher Examples**
- Trying out a new grading software to speed up your process
- Asking colleagues for feedback on a lesson

**Student Examples**
- Asking for help when needed
- Joining a school club even if you don't know anyone in it

**How do I know?**
The **potential costs** to me or others outweigh the potential benefits.

**Teacher Examples**
- Taking students on a spur-of-the-moment field trip, without obtaining permission slips or notifying the principal
- Deciding not to try out a new and promising instructional technique because you fear it may not work

**Student Examples**
- Cheating on a test
- Avoiding an opportunity to learn something new

**How do I know?**
The potential **benefits** to make a positive contribution **to others** outweigh the potential costs.

**Teacher Examples**
- Trusting your students and yourself to tackle the uncertainty of a complex challenge
- Sharing a new instructional approach you developed at a teaching conference
- Continuing to believe in a student who your colleagues have given up on

**Student Examples**
- Sharing a different way of solving a problem that can contribute to your peers' understanding
- Trying to solve a complex challenge facing your school or community
- Standing with a student who is alone, alienated, or picked on

Note: Thumbs up and down icons were made by Egor Rumyan from www.flaticon.com

Figure 1.1.   Different Types of Risks

Beautiful risks refer to having the courage to think and act in ways that go beyond oneself. They represent actions—big or small—that have the potential to make a new and positive contribution to the learning and life of others. There are numerous iconic examples of people taking beautiful risks that have changed the course of history (e.g., Rosa Parks, Mahatma Gandhi, the "tank man" protester in Tiananmen Square).

Legendary and historic examples of beautiful risk taking are inspirational and highlight how a seemingly small, albeit potentially costly, action can make an immensely positive and lasting contribution. In the context of the classroom, seemingly small actions, with even seemingly low potential costs, can also make important and lasting contributions (Beghetto, 2016a).

Sharing a new instructional approach that you developed at a national teaching conference is a beautiful risk. Trusting your students and yourself to start a T-shirt business aimed at promoting awareness of issues facing teens is another example. Even something as seemingly simple as continuing to believe in a student who your colleagues have given up on is a beautiful risk. All involve potential hazards, but also stand the chance to make a positive contribution to others.

You can also encourage and recognize the beautiful risks your students take each day. Whether it is sitting with another student who everyone ignores in the lunchroom or sharing a different perspective on a topic that can help promote understanding, all students are capable of taking beautiful risks. Most simply need opportunities, examples, and reinforcement for doing so.

Although all students are capable of beautiful risks, they likely will need your help differentiating amongst different kinds of risks. You can help by spending time briefly highlighting the different types and generating examples of what these risks look like in their everyday lives. This includes providing reminders and encouraging students to engage in both good and beautiful risk taking.

## TAKING BEAUTIFUL RISKS

One way to think about beautiful risks is that they serve as a bridge between planned actions and making creative contributions to others. Because uncertainty is involved in taking beautiful risks, there are potential hazards that you need to consider in addition to the potential benefits. These considerations are illustrated in figure 1.2. As depicted in figure 1.2, taking beautiful risks requires trying to anticipate, minimize, and address the potential hazards en route to making a creative contribution to others. Doing so involves:

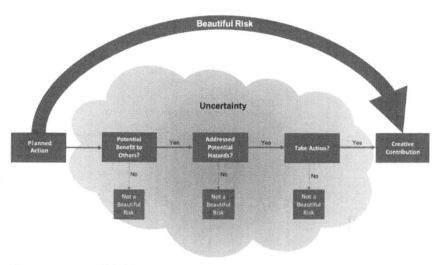

**Figure 1.2.   Beautiful Risks as a Bridge**

- determining whether the action you plan to take will potentially benefit others,
- identifying and planning how to work through potential hazards, and
- taking action.

Taking a beautiful risk does not, of course, guarantee a creative outcome. But unless we and our students are willing to take such risks, then creative contributions to others are not possible. Therefore, even if a beautiful risk doesn't turn out in the way we hope it will, it is still worth taking because the potential benefits to others are greater than the potential hazards. And we can always learn from the process.

Indeed, in the context of the classroom, taking beautiful risks is a learning opportunity. When you and your students take a beautiful risk, no matter what the outcome, there is always an opportunity to learn from it. Doing so requires reflecting on what went well, what could have been done differently, and how to move forward.

Even with the positive social and individual benefits that can come from taking beautiful risks, you and your students may still fear the potential consequences of this form of risk-taking. Unless you work through this fear, it will get in the way of taking action when it is beneficial and *necessary* to do so. So, how might you do this?

One way is to establish a trusting environment, conducive to risk taking. Indeed, one of the most common ways of thinking about productive risk taking is: If we build a trusting environment, then people will be willing to take risks. In actuality, it's just the opposite. As Wharton psychologist Adam Grant and author Daniel Coyle have explained:

> [Grant:] I've always thought about trust as the willingness to be vulnerable and take a risk together, but you convinced me that I had it backward. . . . You [Coyle] said, "Actually, *you take risks together first*, and that's how you build trust. (Grant & Coyle, 2018, italics added)

As the above excerpt highlights, building the trust necessary for beautiful risk-taking in your classroom starts with you and your students taking beautiful risks together. Put simply: If you want your students to develop their willingness to take beautiful risks, then require them to take such risks.

The vulnerability and learning that comes from taking beautiful risks will go a long way in building a trusting classroom environment. This is not to say that there's no benefit in preparing your students and yourself for taking beautiful risks. Indeed, it's actually quite helpful to get clear on the action you plan on taking, the potential hazards, and the potential benefits to others prior to taking the beautiful risk. But, ultimately, you still need to take the risk.

In some cases, running through these considerations will occur "on the fly"—taking no more than a few seconds or minutes prior to taking action. Deciding to take class time to explore a surprising idea offered by a student during a class discussion is an example. Prior to exploring the idea, it's beneficial to first quickly weigh the amount of class time it would take to explore that idea against the potential benefits to the class conversation.

In situations where you have more time to act, it's always beneficial to slow down and carefully consider the action you plan to take and the potential outcomes of that action. Let's explore an example. Imagine you want to provide your students with an opportunity to apply what they are learning to a problem they have identified in their school or community.

You have never tried something like this before, but you believe doing so will help them put their learning to creative use and also benefit members of the community. You do not have a lot of time to devote to this project but can likely spend twenty minutes each Monday on it. Given you've never done something like this before and because you only have a limited amount of time to devote to it, you feel apprehensive.

Part of you worries that launching a complex project like this may not work and that you should wait until next year. But another part of you feels like if you don't start now, you'll never do it and your students will miss out on an important learning opportunity. You feel stuck—caught between doing nothing and facing the uncertainty of taking action.

In a situation such as this one, it can be helpful to use a simple checklist to think through the action you are about to take. Checklists can be beneficial in helping manage complexity (Gawande, 2009) and guide you through the uncertainty of preparing to take a beautiful risk. In addition to helping you prepare and decide whether to take a beautiful risk, they can also be helpful in supporting your learning after you take such risks.

Figure 1.3 is an example of a beautiful risk checklist, which includes two parts. The first part includes questions to work through before taking action and the second part includes items that will help you and your students reflect on the outcome and learn from the experience.

Whenever you are planning on launching a new curricular activity or project, it can be beneficial to use the beautiful risk checklist (figure 1.3) to help you and your students think through the actions you plan to take. Including your students in the checklist process can help cultivate a classroom environment that expects and encourages beautiful risks. Indeed, one of the best ways to develop new behaviors in your students is to model those behaviors yourself (Bandura, 1997).

Launching a new learning experience, like the hypothetical Monday project described above, represents a perfect opportunity to discuss the concept of beautiful risks with your students. You can start by letting them know that you will be trying something that you haven't done before, but that you think will be an exciting and meaningful learning experience.

You can then discuss how trying something new is "a bit risky" and then, if you haven't already, discuss the different types of risks (good, bad, and beautiful). Next, you can use the checklist in figure 1.3 to have a guided discussion of what specifically the action entails, the input you have received (or need to obtain) from others, and how you might monitor progress along the way.

You can also spend time discussing and clarifying the potential benefits to others, including who likely will benefit most from the action and what specific outcomes you anticipate from taking the action. Next you can spend time discussing potential hazards involved in taking the action. What are those hazards and who might they impact if left unaddressed?

In addition to clarifying the potential hazards, you and your students can discuss ways you can avoid or at least minimize those hazards. This discussion also includes seeking input from others (e.g., colleagues, school administration, partners in the community) to identify potential pitfalls and considerations that you and your students might be missing.

Depending on the duration of the action you are taking, you may need to make adjustments along the way. This is why establishing a plan for how you will monitor progress is so important. By monitoring progress, you can be ready to respond to any unanticipated challenges that emerge and be in a

| BEAUTIFUL RISK CHECKLIST |
|---|
| **BEFORE TAKING ACTION** |

*Action to Be Taken:*

- ☐ Are you clear on the action you want to take?
- ☐ Have you obtained input from others?
- ☐ How might you monitor progress on the actions you take (so you can make "as-needed" changes)?

*Potential Benefits to Others:*

- ☐ Will this action benefit others?
- ☐ Who will most benefit from this action?
- ☐ What are some of those benefits?

*Potential Hazards:*

- ☐ What are some potential hazards to taking action?
- ☐ Have you obtained input from others on potential hazards you may not be considering?
- ☐ Who might these hazards impact?
- ☐ How might you avoid or minimize those hazards?
- ☐ How might you monitor progress?

**AFTER TAKING ACTION**

*Outcome*

- ☐ What was the outcome of taking the action?
- ☐ Did it result in a creative contribution to others?
- ☐ What was different about the result than you expected?
- ☐ What went well and not so well?
- ☐ What additional actions might be needed?

*Reflection*

- ☐ What would you do differently if you had the opportunity to take the action again?
- ☐ What did you learn from taking this action?
- ☐ How will what you learned from this experience inform your actions moving forward?

Figure 1.3.   Beautiful Risk Checklist

better position to address them (Beghetto, 2016a). When working in a context of uncertainty, the one thing you can be certain of is that surprises will emerge. It is therefore important for you and your students to expect the unexpected.

After you have taken action, you and your students can return to the checklist to help guide your reflection on what actually occurred and what you learned from the experience. Taking beautiful risks in an educational context is all about learning. As such, no matter what the outcome, you and your students can still learn about the experience.

Bringing students into the pre- and post-action thinking that goes into taking beautiful risks will teach them how they can run through a similar process whenever they plan to take action. You can have them use (or modify) the checklist in figure 1.3 to become familiar with the kinds of things they should consider whenever they take beautiful risks—regardless of whether it requires taking a more immediate or longer-term action.

## SUMMARIZING ACTION PRINCIPLE

*If* **you want to establish a classroom conducive to creative teaching and learning,** *then* **you need to help your students differentiate between good, bad, and beautiful risks.**

Teaching and learning creatively is risky. There are hazards involved whenever we try to think and act in new ways. But the risks involved in creative teaching and learning represent beautiful risks, because the potential benefits to others tend to outweigh the costs. Even so, we may still fear taking such risks.

When fear guides our actions, we miss out on important opportunities and responsibilities to make positive and lasting contributions to others. An initial step we can take to address the fear that comes with beautiful risk-taking is to work through the action we plan to take. The beautiful risk checklist (figure 1.3) introduced earlier in this chapter can help guide you and your students through the planning process of taking beautiful risks.

Recall, the best way to work through the fear and build the trust necessary for taking beautiful risks is to take those risks together (Grant & Coyle, 2018). Moreover, we can also remind ourselves and our students that even if a beautiful risk doesn't work out we can still learn from the process.

The remaining chapters in this book focus on particular beautiful risks you and your students can take to increase the chances that you'll make creative contributions in and beyond the classroom. By taking beautiful risks together you will also bolster the courage and confidence necessary to step into uncertainty and take creative action in a way that complements and enhances teaching and learning.

*Chapter Two*

# The Beautiful
# Risk of a Creative Classroom

You can't use up creativity. The more you use, the more you have.

—Maya Angelou

Inviting creativity into your classroom takes courage. It requires being willing to step into the unknown, confront uncertainty, and think and act in different ways. This can be particularly challenging in light of how we tend experience classroom teaching and learning. Indeed, schools often privilege sameness, not difference (Glăveanu & Beghetto, 2016).

Students typically are expected to learn the same thing, at the same time, and in the same way. Students are then expected to provide the same answers, to the same problems, using the same procedures (Beghetto, 2018). Although an emphasis on sameness can be an efficient way of organizing teaching (Sawyer, 2016), the obvious problem with this approach is it leaves little room for creative expression.

In schools and classrooms that reinforce sameness, even slight differences can really stand out. and typically not in good ways. Consequently, thinking and acting differently comes with its share of hazards. Teachers who try to teach differently run the risk of raising eyebrows and even receiving resistance from their colleagues, students, parents, and administration.

Students who share an unexpected perspective or idea run the risk of being ignored, dismissed, or ridiculed. Creative expression in teaching and learning, however, also has its share of benefits. Creative learning can not only benefit individual students but also contribute to the learning of peers and teachers.

A student who, for instance, shares a unique perspective during a class discussion can provide new ways for her peers and teachers to understand the topic. In this way, student creativity is a beautiful risk because the potential benefits go beyond individual students.

Teaching creatively is also a beautiful risk as it can provide students with new kinds of experiences that enable them to deepen their knowledge and skills. A teacher who, for example, designs a community-based learning experience can help students make a creative contribution to others outside of the classroom.

The purpose of this chapter and the remainder of this book is to help you consider how you might maximize the benefits of establishing a creative classroom, while avoiding potential pitfalls. Doing so starts with understanding what creativity means for your classroom. Indeed, one of the biggest hazards of trying to establish a creative classroom is basing it on an unclear understanding of creativity.

## WHAT IS CREATIVITY?

Everyone has a general idea about creativity. Some people view it as having something to do with the arts. Others might associate it with catchphrases like "thinking outside the box." Still others might believe that it is a thing that some people have, but they themselves do not. In most cases, people associate creativity with some form of original expression. How do you think about creativity?

Let's consider a couple examples.[1] A student is asked to complete a math worksheet that includes various pictures of quadrilaterals (e.g., rectangle, rhombus, parallelogram, square). The student is instructed to name each of the pictured quadrilaterals. In response, the student writes, "Bob," "Sam," "Tedison," and "Cate" in the space under each quadrilateral. Is this a creative response?

Let's consider another example. A student is asked to draw a plant cell and identify its most important parts. In response, the student draws a picture of a flower with a sad face, behind prison bars. The student then labels the "iron bars" and "lack of windows" of the plant's cell. How about this student's response? Is it creative?

If you're like most people, you may chuckle and agree that they are examples of student creativity. Indeed, these seem to be examples of students who are thinking "outside the box." The students are responding in surprising and unexpected ways. So, isn't that what creativity is all about?

What might creativity researchers say? Creativity researchers likely would say the students are clearly demonstrating *originality* in these responses. But, in the context of what the students were asked to do, they're not demonstrating creativity. This is because creativity requires more than originality.

Most definitions of creativity (Plucker, Beghetto, & Dow, 2004; Runco & Jaeger, 2012) tend to involve some combination of: originality *and* meeting task constraints within a particular context.[2] Table 2.1 provides an example of how the components of this definition can be applied to determine whether something would be considered creative.

As displayed in table 2.1, if a student comes up with a highly unusual idea (e.g., an interpretive dance) for a science fair project, but it doesn't meet the preestablished criteria of the science fair, then it would not be considered creative. In another context (e.g., a performance art exhibit), however, that same interpretive dance could be considered creative.

Conversely, if a student shares an example of an experiment from the textbook, it might meet the criteria in the context of a science class discussion, but it wouldn't be considered creative because it lacks originality. This does not diminish the value of such a response. When checking understanding of a concept, having students provide a common example is fine. Not every example or idea needs to be creative.

That said, if we are looking for creativity then the idea needs to both be original and meet the established criteria for the context or task at hand. In this way, a sixth grade student's health-based science fair project would be considered creative in her school science fair.

Take that same creative project outside the sixth grade science fair and it likely would fail to meet the criteria or originality necessary to be considered creative at a professional level. Again, this does not diminish the creativity or value of the student's project in the sixth grade context. It simply illustrates that contextually defined criteria matter when deciding what is and is not creative.

This is not to say that students cannot produce products or innovations that would be considered creative across multiple contexts, including professional contexts. Indeed, the Google Science Fair provides several examples of projects developed by young people that are widely recognized as creative at a professional level (see www.googlesciencefair.com/).

Understanding these components of the definition of creativity will help you and your students recognize what is and is not creative in your classroom and beyond. As will be discussed in the next section and throughout this book, combining originality with existing task constraints can result in more creative teaching and learning outcomes *and* help cultivate a creative mindset that permeates your entire classroom.

The following section will help you and your students build on this definition and use it to take the beautiful risk of establishing a creative classroom.

**Table 2.1.**

APPLYING THE COMPONENTS OF CREATIVITY

| Example | What is the context? | What are the criteria? | Is it original? | Does it meet the predetermined criteria? | Is it creative? |
|---|---|---|---|---|---|
| 1. A student's interpretive dance of photosynthesis | 6th grade science fair | Design an experiment or project that demonstrates a scientific concept | Yes | No | No |
| 2. A student's interpretive dance of photosynthesis | 6th grade performance art exhibit | Communicate an idea, concept, or emotion using the performing arts | Yes | Yes | **Yes** |
| 3. A student shares an example from the textbook | 6th grade science class discussion | Provide an example of an experiment | No | Yes | No |
| 4. A student designs and conducts her own unique health sciences experiment | 6th grade science fair | Design your own experiment or project that demonstrates a scientific concept | Yes | Yes | **Yes** |
| 5. A student designs and conducts her own health sciences experiment | National Institute of Health research competition | Submit a grant proposal to a Federal Health Institute that funds large-scale, scientific research studies in the health sciences | No | No | No |

## TAKING THE BEAUTIFUL RISK

In most educational contexts, the kinds of experiences we present to students tend to have clearly defined criteria. As the definition of creativity introduced in the previous section highlights, having clearly defined task constraints does not stifle creativity, but rather is *necessary* for creative expression in educational contexts. Indeed, creativity thrives in constraints (Beghetto, 2017a; Stokes, 2006, 2010).

If you have clearly defined task constraints, then you're already halfway to a creative classroom. All that is needed is to add a bit of originality. Put simply, classroom creativity involves meeting criteria, but doing so in a new or different way. The existing goals, priorities, and outcomes of your classroom serve as the criteria. And the originality comes from finding new and different ways to meet those criteria.

Taking the beautiful risk of establishing a creative classroom requires anticipating and addressing some common hazards when it comes to beliefs and conceptions about creativity. Let's take a closer look at some of these hazards and explore how the definition can help minimize the hazards and, at the same time, maximize the benefits of taking this beautiful risk.

### Avoiding the Originality Hazard

We've already touched on this hazard, but because it is so common and persistent it is worth a bit more discussion. As mentioned, this hazard pertains to viewing originality and creativity as the same thing. Doing so is not surprising given that originality and creativity sometimes appear as synonyms in dictionaries and thesauruses. Researchers who have looked at how people define creativity have also noted that originality tends to be the most important or easily recognized feature of those definitions (Plucker et al., 2004; Runco & Charles, 1993).

Helping your students understand that *creativity is more than originality* (Beghetto, 2013) will help ensure that they recognize that while they may be asked to come up with a new or different way of doing things, they still need to meet the criteria, guidelines, and expectations of that assignment. This will also help address the common misconception that creativity involves a negative form of deviance, eccentricity, and disruptive behavior (Feist, 1998; Plucker et al., 2004).

Creative thought and action can, of course, be put to harmful ends. People sometimes engage in negative and even destructive forms of creative behavior (Cropley, Cropley, Kaufman, & Runco, 2010), such as coming up with novel ways to break agreed-upon rules, commit crimes, and harm others. This is why it is important to help define, with your students, what the expectations are for creative thought and action in your classroom.

You can also help your students understand when it is and is not beneficial to act differently by helping them learn how to evaluate a situation and determine whether creativity is necessary (Kaufman & Beghetto, 2013). Indeed, there are many times when following the routine in an expected way is not only preferable, but necessary.

If, for instance, you're teaching students safety procedures in the science lab, you would want them to adhere to those procedures rather than try to come up with their own way of doing things. Helping students differentiate between situations that require a more standardized approach versus those that benefit from multiple ways of doing things can help them successfully share their own unique perspectives and act in new ways.

It all starts with recognizing that creativity is not the same thing as originality. Classroom creativity requires the situational awareness of knowing when and how to do something different that still meets the criteria for the task at hand (Kaufman & Beghetto, 2013). Helping students recognize appropriate openings for expressing their originality can help ensure that creative thought and action has a meaningful place in your classroom.

## Avoiding the Arts Hazard

When you think of creativity do you think of the arts? If so, you're not alone. Many people associate creativity with the arts (Glăveanu, 2011). This makes sense because the arts enable people to explore and represent new and different possibilities (Greene, 1995).

The problem with this arts-based association—similar to the problem with the originality hazard—is when the association morphs from seeing the arts as representing *one way* of expressing creativity into *the only way*. This limited conception is particularly problematic in the classroom.

If your students believe that the only way to engage in creative expression is to incorporate the arts into everything they do, then it can quickly become overwhelming and counterproductive. This is not to say that mash-ups between academic subject matter and the arts can't lead to creative expression. They certainly can.

Many teachers have used or developed lessons that blend artistic design and academic topics or concepts (e.g., visual representations of mathematical concepts). The results can be quite creative and aesthetically pleasing. Inviting creativity into your classroom, however, does not require using the arts.

Creativity can be infused into any academic subject area (Renzulli, 2016). A student who comes up with a novel idea for a living history project in social studies is an example. Another example would be a student's unexpected yet mathematically accurate way of solving a math story problem.

Creativity typically looks different in different activities and subject areas, but as long as there is an opening for novel and meaningful expression, creativity is possible. In this way, creative blends between academic learning and other things (e.g., students' interests, skills of family members, expertise of people in the community) can also yield creative outcomes (Beghetto & Breslow, 2017).

When teaching a lesson on ratios you can have students list their interests (e.g., cooking, a particular video game, fashion, swimming). You can then teach them what a ratio is and have them work alone or in teams to combine their understanding of a ratio with their interest. Each group can then demonstrate the novel ratios they developed in their particular interest area.

The key consideration for avoiding the arts hazard, therefore, is to help your students recognize that creativity can be expressed in most any human endeavor (Kaufman, 2016) or academic subject area (Renzulli, 2016), which includes but is not limited to the arts.

## Avoiding the Fixed Trait Hazard

How we talk about creativity matters. It is easy to inadvertently describe it as a fixed trait, which some people or things possess, and others do not. Consider the following statements:

- "Sophia is a very creative student, Ronnie is not."
- "Your bulletin boards scream creativity! Mine look like a robot made them."
- "Some of our colleagues are such creative teachers, I'm just not one of them."

Comments like those above often go by without any further discussion or consideration. These kinds of statements and ways of thinking about creativity are problematic for a variety of reasons.

First, just like fixed beliefs about ability can unnecessarily stifle learning and competence development (Dweck, 2006), students who believe creativity is a fixed trait can similarly undermine our efforts to incorporate it into our classrooms (see Karwowski, 2014). The way we and others talk about creativity can influence what our students believe about creativity.

If your students do not believe they can think and act creatively, then it is unlikely that they will take the risk of trying (Karwowski & Beghetto, 2018).

Not only is this a missed opportunity, it can actually be a hazard in itself. Indeed, failing to share ideas or take actions when they can benefit others because our students do not believe in the creative potential of their ideas can be harmful.

A student who, for instance, has a unique idea for how to disrupt the increasingly hateful bullying of other students needs to feel encouraged and supported in taking the beautiful risk of developing and taking action on that idea. Otherwise the situation can get worse. Developing and taking action on potentially creative ideas is therefore a responsibility that we all share.

Another problem with viewing creativity as a fixed trait is students may assume that a person who has demonstrated high levels of creativity in one activity or subject area will automatically be willing and able to demonstrate high levels of creativity across all subject areas or activities. Although it may be possible to demonstrate creativity in various domains, doing so requires developing the skills, knowledge, and interest in each of those domains (Baer, 2015).

One way to think about this is to recognize that there are different levels of creative expression, which range from our own personal insights and experiences to historic contributions (Beghetto & Kaufman, 2007; Cohen, 1989; Runco, 1996; Stein, 1953, 1987). These different levels have been described elsewhere as the *Four C model* of creativity (Kaufman & Beghetto, 2009) and include:

- *mini-c creativity (self-recognized)*—new and meaningful individual experiences, insight, observations, or interpretations that we have in learning and life (e.g., a teacher coming up with a new idea for a lesson; a student coming up with a new idea for a short story);
- *little-c creativity (recognized by people in your everyday environment)*— creative contributions that others in our immediate or everyday environment recognize as being novel and meeting the constraints of a situation (e.g., a student shares a new way of thinking about a concept that helps other students understand it better);
- *Pro-c creativity (recognized by professionals and experts)*—creative contributions that experts in particular areas recognize as being unique and relevant (e.g., a teacher shares at national conference a new way of using video to improve student engagement during social studies instruction); and
- *Big-C creativity (historical and lasting recognition)*—legendary and lasting creative contributions that have been recognized by historians, scholars, experts, and practitioners as making a revolutionary or transformative contribution (e.g., the concept of kindergarten introduced by Friedrich Froebel).

The Four Cs can help you and your students talk about the level of creativity that makes sense for your classroom. In most cases, mini-c and little-c likely will be the focus. Indeed, learning creatively (Beghetto, 2016b) involves developing new and personally meaningful insights (mini-c), which can be tested out and shared with others.

By having students share their mini-c insights, they have an opportunity to deepen their own personal understanding and potentially make a little-c contribution to the learning and understanding of others (see also chapter 4). A goal for your classroom therefore would be aimed at encouraging your students to share and develop their emerging ideas and perspectives (mini-c) into school or classroom level contributions (little-c).

We can help avoid the hazard of fixed trait beliefs about creativity by continually reminding ourselves and our students that all people are capable of demonstrating creativity, but doing so requires effort, knowledge of the task, and support. This includes recognizing that there are different levels of creative expression.

Whereas we have mini-c moments on a daily basis, performing at the little-c level takes practice and feedback. Moreover, Pro-c level creativity requires many years of deliberate practice. Pro-c creativity requires having the expertise and access to expert judges and professional communities who can recognize these types of creative contributions. Big-C creativity is essentially out of the hands of the creator and is bestowed on these contributions after they have stood the test of time (Kaufman & Beghetto, 2009).

In short, students can benefit from recognizing that creativity is a capacity they all have. And, depending on the type of contribution they want to make (i.e., the level of the Four Cs), its expression can range from experiences that they routinely have in their everyday learning to contributions that require many, many years of deliberate practice.

## Avoiding the Magical Technique Hazard

Trying something new in your classroom can be intimidating. It is therefore understandable to look for some kind of magical creativity technique that will offer a step-by-step guide to building a creative classroom. Any new technique or technology that promises enhancing creativity can therefore be quite tempting.

Creativity researchers have long recognized this temptation. As Frank Barron (1969) explained many decades ago, those of us who are "genuinely interested in creativity as an educational goal" are tempted to seek out or hope for some "packaged method for stimulating creative processes" (p. 2).

Unfortunately, there are no prepackaged methods that guarantee classroom creativity. Rather, creative expression in your classroom will come from providing openings that invite you and your students to think and act in different ways while still adhering to the guidelines and criteria you have established. The remaining chapters in this book provide examples and suggestions.

This is not to say that strategies and techniques for increasing the chances of creative thought are not available. Indeed, there are various promising examples of thinking strategies and programs (Isaksen & Treffinger, 2004; Nickerson, 1999; Scott et al., 2004). Perhaps one of the most widely used classroom creativity techniques is SCAMPER (Eberle, 1996).

SCAMPER refers to **s**ubstitute, **c**ombine, **a**dapt, **m**odify, **p**ut to another use, **e**liminate, and **r**everse. Each of these verbs can be applied to a situation or task to help students think about it in a new way. Doing so *can* lead to new and relevant (i.e., creative) insights.

You might, for instance, invite your students to *substitute* the ending of one story with the ending of another, resulting in a potentially creative mash-up. The simple strategy of *combining* academic topics with student interests, described earlier, is another example of how you can use one of these verbs to generate potentially new ways of promoting deeper understanding of a concept.

It's not that the SCAMPER verbs are somehow filled with magical creativity dust. Rather, they are based on the basic understanding that creativity benefits from challenging assumptions and coming up with new ways of thinking (Beghetto, 2016a). You can easily come up with your own acronyms or verbs, which may be equally effective, such as BAM.

BAM could stand for **b**ig is small, **a**cceptable is harmful, **m**ore is less (or vice versa). You and your students might use the BAM acronym to challenge assumptions about a complex social situation your class is trying to solve. A big problem may actually be smaller than you think. Something that has been acceptable in the past is now considered harmful. Doing more of a seemingly good thing may start to erode its value.

Regardless of the words you use to help promote new ways of thinking, students will still need to make a meaningful connection to the goals, criteria, and guidelines of the specific activity in order for it to be considered creative. In this way, no matter how promising a strategy or technique, there are no guarantees that it will result in creative outcomes.

The key is to understand the basic principle of what determines whether something would be considered creative in your classroom. Specifically, it would need to be a different or new way of meeting the particular goals, instructions, or academic criteria that you have established for the task or assignment.

In order to avoid the magical technique hazard, it is important that we and our students resist the temptation to put too much value in any specific technique or strategy. Instead, we can recognize that regardless of the specific activities or techniques we use to promote new ways of thinking, we will still have to tailor them to our specific situation, instructional goals, and curricular responsibilities.

## Avoiding the Creative Product Hazard

Inherent in the conception of creativity is the requirement of ultimately producing something. Creators create. A creative insight, no matter how fantastic, has little value to others if it never sees the light of day (Beghetto, 2016a). Consequently, tangible products are the clearest example of creative production. Without a tangible end product, it is difficult to determine whether something or someone is creative (Plucker et al., 2004).

In fact, one of the most frequently used forms of creativity assessment involves having experts judge creative products (Amabile, 1996). This approach is straightforward and rather elegant. It can be described in two simple steps (Baer & McKool, 2009, p. 4):

1. People are asked to create something (e.g., a drawing, a poem, a scientific study), and
2. A small group of relevant experts independently evaluate the creativity of those products.

If, for instance, a researcher wants to assess the creativity of poems written by a group of college students, then the researcher can use this approach to assemble a panel of published poets to independently judge the creativity demonstrated in those poems. When using this approach, researchers have found that the reliability amongst expert raters tends to be quite high and the validity comes from the expertise of the raters (Baer & McKool, 2009).

Research based on this approach has also helped to demonstrate that just because a person can write a poem deemed creative by a panel of judges, doesn't mean that same person can draw a picture that will also be rated highly (Baer, 2016). In this way, having people create something tangible has played a key role in creativity research.

Having your students create things is important and does have value. And much can be learned from transforming an idea into a tangible product. That said, students are still in the process of developing their creative competence and likely will benefit more from reflecting and receiving feedback on the *process* than on the product.

Indeed, just because expert assessment of creative products is an important part of creativity research does not mean that it makes sense for your classroom. Bringing together a panel of judges to assess the relative creativity of what your students produce is completely unnecessary. As will be discussed in chapter 7, there are various ways you can assess student creativity in your everyday classroom that are much less resource intensive.

On occasion, some of your students may produce work that would benefit from receiving expert critique and recognition (e.g., submitting a short story to a writing contest or for publication). In such cases, it would make sense to encourage and support them in pushing their work out into the world. Doing so includes preparing them to learn from set backs and difficult-to-hear feedback (see chapter 7).

The kinds of support you provide in your everyday classroom can be as, or more, important than these less frequent occasions. We should therefore help our students recognize that creating tangible products is only a small part of the process. And just because they have not been viewed as creative by some expert audience (Runco, 2005) does not mean that they lack creative potential.

As discussed in chapter 1, we can all learn from the process of taking creative risks. Even if the process results in failure, mistakes, or no tangible product. Given that learning is the primary goal of school, the focus should be on what is learned from the process with an eye on how that learning can be applied in the future. If the focus is only on what is produced, then it is easy to overlook key learning opportunities.

## SUMMARIZING ACTION PRINCIPLE

*If* **you want to cultivate a creative classroom,** *then* **developing a clear understanding of what creativity means for your classroom is an essential first step toward taking this beautiful risk.**

Developing a creative classroom has the benefit of enriching the teaching and learning that is already occurring in your classroom. Doing so requires being aware of the potential hazards that come from too narrow of a conception of what creativity means.

Specifically, classroom creativity is all about creating opportunities for you and your students to engage in original thought and action while still meeting the task constraints, guidelines, and academic goals of a particular activity or assignment.

By developing your students' understanding of what creativity means for your classroom, you'll be ready to transform potential hazards into powerful opportunities for creative expression. It all starts with a recognition that classroom creativity is more than originality, more than the arts, more than a magical technique, and more than a product. It is an opportunity, a responsibility, and a potential that we can all realize.

We can also support classroom creativity by helping our students recognize that creative expression is not always necessary or beneficial. Indeed, a sign of an accomplished creator is knowing when and when not to be creative (Kaufman & Beghetto, 2013).

One way to support creative expression, therefore, involves helping students carefully consider the criteria and expectations of a particular learning situation and deciding whether the benefits of taking creative action outweigh potential hazards.

The remaining chapters of this book build on the definition and ideas introduced here and provide more specific ideas, examples, and insights for how you and your students can take the kinds of beautiful risks necessary to establish a creative classroom.

## NOTES

1. These examples are based on popular Internet memes of student work.

2. This is not to say that all creativity researchers are in perfect agreement about the definitional criteria of creativity (see, for instance, Corrazza, 2016; Simonton, 2017; Smith & Smith, 2017). Specific aspects and nuances of the definition likely will continue to be discussed for the foreseeable future. Most creativity scholars, however, tend to agree that creativity involves some blend of originality, uniqueness, novelty, newness *and* meaningfulness, usefulness, and meeting tasking constraints (Beghetto, 2013; Kaufman, 2016; Plucker et al., 2004; Runco & Jaeger, 2012).

## Chapter Three

# The Beautiful Risk
# of Embracing Uncertainty

I have seen what could be and asked why not.

—Pablo Picasso

Learning and life are filled with uncertainty (Byrnes, 2011). Just because we frequently experience uncertainty doesn't mean that we like it. Indeed, most of us like stable routines and habits. This is because consistency is comfortable and reassuring. Consistency and clarity are particularly important in the classroom.

As teachers we spend a lot of time carefully planning lessons and clearly communicating our expectations to students. This is because we recognize that classroom uncertainty can quickly turn into student frustration, disengagement, and disruptions (Skinner & Belmont, 1993).

In this way, much of what we do when planning lessons and developing classroom routines is to remove or at least significantly reduce uncertainty (Beghetto, 2016a; Clark, 1983; Callahan, Saye, & Brush, 2014; Leikin & Kawass, 2005). This involves establishing clear expectations, well-defined criteria, and helpful guidelines (Jang, Reeve, & Deci, 2010). A classroom that lacks this basic structure is a classroom on the brink of disarray.

Uncertainty, when viewed from this perspective, appears to be a hazard that should be avoided rather than embraced. Although classroom uncertainty can be problematic, not all uncertainty we face in the classroom is the same (Beghetto, 2018). And, as will be discussed, when it comes to creative teaching and learning, some amount of uncertainty is actually necessary. So how might you take the beautiful risk of welcoming uncertainty in your classroom to support creative teaching and learning, while at the same time avoiding the hazards?

The purpose of this chapter is address this question by clarifying when and how uncertainty can be used to support creative expression in your classroom.

# THE CONNECTION
# BETWEEN UNCERTAINTY AND CREATIVITY

In most cases it is often beneficial and necessary for your students to adhere to well-established academic procedures and behavioral routines. Not only are these procedures and routines efficient, they are also one of the most effective ways of dealing with common tasks and activities. There is no need to introduce uncertainty into such situations.

Your students, for instance, do not need to come up with their own creative way of using well-established academic procedures, like using coordinates on a map to find a specific location, using a particular format for taking notes, or how to use the standard order of operations to simply expressions.

Similarly, you likely don't want to leave it up to your students to come up with their own way of taking the stage for a school concert or finding their own unique path for exiting the building during a fire drill. That said, there are times when routine ways of dealing with a situation no longer work (Beghetto, 2016a). If during an actual fire the exit is blocked, we want to be able to have the confidence to explore new options.

Moreover, there are also times when it may be beneficial to develop new and different ways of thinking or acting. If a schoolwide antibullying program is no longer working because kids are using more covert and technology-based bullying tactics, then we want our students and colleagues to be able to come up with creative ways of thinking about and addressing the problem.

In such cases, having the confidence and willingness to respond creatively to uncertainty is beneficial. If we want to help our students (and ourselves) develop the confidence necessary to successfully navigate uncertainty in and outside of school, then we need to provide them with opportunities to do so in a supportive and well-defined learning environment (Beghetto, 2018).

## Different Types of Uncertainty

If you have ever taught a lesson without adequate preparation or taught a group of students when there is no established set of procedures or expectations, you know how uncomfortable and chaotic the situation can become. If students do not know what is expected of them or how they can find help if they need it, then they are more likely to experience frustration, disengage, and even act out (Skinner & Belmont, 1993).

Although it is true that uncertainty can result in curricular disarray, it is also true that uncertainty presents an opportunity to think and act differently. As I have discussed elsewhere (Beghetto, 2016a; 2018), the key is to recognize that not all uncertainty is the same. Indeed, there are at least four different types of uncertainty you and your students can experience in the classroom: *chaotic uncertainty, stacked uncertainty, encountered uncertainty,* and *planned uncertainty.*

Each of these four forms is summarized in table 3.1 and briefly discussed in the sections that follow.

In the sections that follow, we'll take a closer look at the forms of uncertainty represented in table 3.1, starting with the two that pose the greatest hazards: chaotic uncertainty and stacked uncertainty. And we'll close with a discussion of the two types of uncertainty that represent beautiful risks: encountered uncertainty and planned uncertainty.

## Chaotic Uncertainty

Chaotic uncertainty results from a learning environment characterized by contradictory expectations, unclear guidelines, and confusing criteria for success (Jang, Reeve, & Deci, 2010). Chaotic learning environments introduce

**Table 3.1.   Four Types of Uncertainty**

| Type of Uncertainty | Characteristics | Type of Risk | Avoid or Embrace? |
|---|---|---|---|
| Chaotic Uncertainty | Inconsistent or contradictory expectations <br> Unclear guidelines <br> Confusing criteria for success | Bad Risk | Avoid |
| Stacked Uncertainty | Complex and ill-defined learning tasks, plus <br> Inconsistent or contradictory expectations <br> Unclear guidelines <br> Confusing criteria for success | Bad Risk | Avoid |
| Encountered Uncertainty | Surprising moments that emerge in a planned lesson <br> Learning environment is structured and supportive | Beautiful Risk | Embrace |
| Planned Uncertainty | Lesson designed with to-be-determined aspects <br> Clear expectations, well-defined criteria <br> Supportive environment | Beautiful Risk | Embrace |

a problematic form of uncertainty that can result in a variety of negative and unexpected student and teacher reactions, including: frustration, anger, disengagement, and disruptive behaviors.

These negative behaviors and experiences can turn into a cycle of negative teacher-student interactions that impede student learning and creative expression. Researchers have, for instance, documented how negative student reactions to a chaotic learning environment can influence negative teacher reactions, which in turn can intensify negative student behaviors (Skinner & Belmont, 1993).

Given the hazards of this form of uncertainty, it represents a bad risk that should be avoided. The primary way of avoiding these hazards is to ensure that you and your students establish a structured and supportive learning environment, which is characterized by clear and consistent expectations, helpful guidance, and well-established criteria for success.

## *Stacked Uncertainty*

Stacked uncertainty results from a complex challenge that students are asked to tackle in a learning environment that lacks a clear and supportive structure. These kinds of experiences are bad risks because they pile uncertainty on top of uncertainty, which can devolve into chaos (Beghetto, 2018).

Here's an example. Imagine a colleague who wants to encourage students creativity by having them come up with an invention that solves a real-world problem. On the surface, this may seem like a good opportunity for students to engage with the uncertainty of identifying a real-world problem and then designing an innovative approach to solve it. In an effort to maximize creativity and student-centered learning, your colleague decides that the students should be in charge of every aspect of the project.

Although this type of project can serve as a vehicle for creative learning (see chapter 5 and Beghetto 2018), adding this kind of uncertainty on top of the uncertainty of unclear criteria, missing guidelines, and lacking supports is a recipe for suppressing student creativity, not supporting it.

Chaotic learning experiences suppress creative expression because they lack clear criteria and support necessary for successfully completing the task. Recall from chapter 2, classroom creativity involves doing things differently while still meeting the established criteria. If the criteria are not clear, then it becomes difficult (if not impossible) for creative expression.

Consequently, such an assignment likely will cause students to feel frustrated and not capable of creative work. This is particularly problematic because students may internalize the failure as a personal deficit (e.g., "I'm not smart or creative enough to do this!").

Moreover, the teacher may feel that such activities are not worth the effort or students are not capable of successfully completing such tasks (e.g., "That was a disaster, that's the last time I try that!" or "I guess my students are not ready for this kind of creative work"), rather than a problem with how the learning activity was designed.

## Encountered Uncertainty

Encountered uncertainty refers to surprising moments that emerge in planned lessons, which occur in an otherwise structured and supportive learning environment. Examples include everything from a student sharing an unexpected idea to a surprising in-the-moment insight you have about taking a lesson in a new direction.

Engaging with this form of uncertainty, in the context of a clearly defined lesson or activity, can result in beneficial, creative learning outcomes (see also chapter 4). This is because such moments invite you and your students to explore, learn, and experience something new, while still trying to make a meaningful connection to the existing goals of the planned lesson.

A math teacher from China describes how the potential benefits of taking this kind of risk can outweigh the potential hazards:

> If the teacher can nicely integrate the unexpectedly emerging events into a planned lesson, this can make the instructional coherence really helpful for student learning. (Cai, Ding, & Want, 2014, p. 276)

The key is integrating these moments into your existing or broader learning goals. Here's an example of how this might look in a classroom, described in Jurow and Creighton (2005):

> In a whole-class discussion of how potential energy is transformed into kinetic energy, Ms. Rivera used a schematic drawing of a rollercoaster to show students the point at which such a transformation would take place. She guided a student's finger along the incline of the rollercoaster and at the top of the first "hill," she stopped and pointed out that this is where potential energy is transformed into kinetic energy. A student commented that it was "just like" when they run on a hill located next to the school. (p. 281)

In this moment, the teacher was inspired by the student's connection between the academic concept and his personal experience. She recognized that an impromptu trip to the hill would be a great way for the entire class to make the connection between potential and kinetic energy for themselves (Jurow & Creighton, 2005).

The teacher worked with the unexpected student response and incorporated it into a highly structured creative activity that connected to and elaborated on the academic concept being taught (i.e., how potential energy is transformed into kinetic energy). In fact, when her students were running up and down the outside hill, she had them use the scientific terminology that they were learning about in class.

Engaging with the uncertainty you encounter as part of an otherwise planned lesson represents a beautiful risk. It does not require physically leaving the classroom (as did Ms. Rivera), but simply being willing to metaphorically step in a new or unexpected direction.

The potential hazard of taking such a risk is that it will disrupt your pre-designed lesson, but the potential benefits come in the form of reinforcing the importance of sharing creative ideas, which can contribute to student and teacher learning. It all comes down to how you navigate such situations so that you and your students can maximize the potential creative benefits of following unexpected moments, without drifting too far afield from your planned lessons (Beghetto, 2013).

Chapter 4 provides a more detailed exploration of the potential benefits and hazards of taking the beautiful risk of "going off script." The important take away for the present discussion is the recognition that engaging with planned uncertainty represents a beautiful risk because of the potential creative learning benefits for you and your students.

## *Planned Uncertainty*

Planned uncertainty refers to learning activities that have clear behavioral expectations, routines, and criteria for success; but intentionally include to-be-determined features (Beghetto, 2018). In this way, planned uncertainty provides students with opportunities for original expression within the limits of your existing learning goals.

Planning for this type of uncertainty is one of the best ways to encourage creative expression in your classroom. Chapters 6 and 8 provide specific guidelines for how you can design and use learning activities with this form of uncertainty. Examples include everything from inviting students to come up with their own topics for a clearly defined research project to asking students to come up with their own way of solving a problem.

Planned uncertainty therefore involves designing learning experiences that provide students with opportunities for creative expression. Such activities represent a blend between predetermined criteria and to-be-determined aspects (Beghetto, 2018). The predetermined criteria are things you would establish in advance of assigning the activity (e.g., topic, amount of time, academic skills to be used, and other guidelines).

The to-be-determined features refer to the things your students need to figure out after receiving the criteria for the assignment. Examples of to-be-determined components can be anything from having students identify a problem to solve, come up with their own way of solving a problem, develop their own solution, or some combination of all three.

Even when providing structure and support, there are still hazards associated with this form of uncertainty. If students are not used to coming up with their own way of doing things, they likely will feel a bit of anxiety and frustration. When providing students with autonomy in their learning, you'll need to continually monitor their experience, so you can provide additional instructional supports as needed.

The key is striking a balance between the extreme ends of the spectrum. Students are not fully autonomous "self-learners" (Kirschner & van Merriënboer, 2013). They are also not completely dependent learners who need instructional spoon-feeding (McKay & Kember, 1997). Rather they need a blend of clear and direct instructional support with some level of autonomy, so they can engage in creative learning.

Striking this balance is necessary for creative learning. This is because creative learning involves developing one's own personal understanding of the preestablished curricula *and* having an opportunity to share their unique perspectives, so they can contribute to the learning of others (Beghetto, 2016b).

By anticipating the need to balance autonomy with instructional support, you'll be ready to provide reassurance and encouragement to students who need it. The more opportunities and practice students have working through uncertainty the more confident and persistent they will become.

## Taking the Beautiful Risk

The primary benefit of welcoming uncertainty into your classroom is that it serves as an opportunity for you and your students to think and act creatively. As long as you have established a clearly defined and instructionally supportive environment, you and your students will be in a position to work positively and productively with uncertainty (Beghetto, 2018).

The following represents a quick summary and checklist of how you can navigate the uncertainty that you encounter and introduce in your classroom. This checklist will also serve as a preview and advanced organizer for the more detailed discussions of how to work productively with uncertainty presented in the chapters 4 and 5.

**Establish and communicate clear criteria and guidelines.** When you design learning activities——especially those that include opportunities for students to respond in their own way—it is important that you establish clear criteria and guidelines.

If, for instance, you're asking students to imagine a hypothetical historical outcome, then you will need to clearly specify the criteria and expectations for doing so (e.g., "Your hypothetical outcome needs to be informed by existing historical sources, it should logically connect to historical antecedents, you can work alone or with a partner, it needs to be compared and contrasted to existing accounts of the event.").

**Acknowledge surprising occurrences and decide how to proceed.** Although it may be tempting to ignore an unexpected response that your students (or you) have during a lesson, it is important to acknowledge these moments and decide how to proceed. Otherwise, you may inadvertently dismiss or dissuade yourself and your students from taking a lesson in a potentially more generative direction.

In some cases, you may decide to return to a surprising response later (e.g., "Olivia brings up an interesting question. We don't have time to go into it today, but I'm going to write it on our "wonder wall" and we'll return to it Friday.").

In other cases, you may decide to take a lesson in a different direction or even stop a lesson that doesn't seem to be working (e.g., "I'm noticing what looks like a lot of frustration and confusion. This activity doesn't seem to be working the way I thought it would . . . let's stop and discuss how we might modify it.").

**Alert students when taking a planned activity in a new direction.** If you decide to take a planned lesson in a new direction, it is important to let your students know that you are doing so. This includes letting students know why you have decided to do so (e.g., "Jasmine brings up an interesting perspective . . . Let's take a few moments and explore this together as it will help us think about this topic in a different way.").

**Highlight relevant guidelines and criteria.** When you decide to take a lesson in a new direction—even if it is a minor detour—it is helpful to establish or reinforce existing guidelines and criteria (e.g., "Ok—we're going to take five minutes to explore Kendrick's idea. You can work with a partner or alone and discuss whether and how Kendrick's idea connects to what we have been discussing.").

**Recognize what was gained (and lost).** When you decide to take a lesson in a new direction, it is important to evaluate the outcomes of doing so. This includes taking a few moments to discuss with your students what you and they feel was gained (and lost) from doing so (e.g., "I didn't plan to spend an extra day exploring this concept, but now that we have let's discuss some of the benefits and drawbacks. Take a few minutes and discuss this with a partner and then I'll invite you to share your ideas and I'll then share mine.").

**Cultivate a +1 mentality.** You can invite new ways of thinking in your lesson by inviting your students to push themselves to come up with as many new and different ways of approaching a task as they can.

If, for instance, you are asking students to generate different ways of solving a story problem and a student comes up with two ways, then ask if they can come up with at least one more way. This kind of +1 mentality will establish an environment where you are continually challenging each other to push the possibilities a bit further.

**Help students make connections.** Whenever you ask students to take charge of their own learning and come up with their own way of completing an assignment or task, it is important to continually ask them how they are making connections to the criteria or goals of the lesson.

Even in relatively brief assignments, it's helpful to have students discuss connections they are making midstream and after they complete the activity:

- *Now that you have had a chance to start working on this, what connections are you making between what you are doing and the topic we've been discussing?*
- *Can you explain how your approach meets the criteria for this assignment?*
- *Describe what you learned from this process.*
- *Describe whether and how it helped you deepen your confidence and understanding of this topic.*

**Have students discuss benefits of how others' ideas impacted them.** Given that beautiful risks are those that make a positive and potentially lasting impact to other people, it is important to make sure that students have an opportunity to discuss and explain how their own and others' ideas have made a positive impact to others:

- *Now that you have had a chance to hear from the other groups, describe whether and how what they did impacted you?*
- *How did your ideas impact others?*
- *How might your ideas be improved upon?*
- *If you were to do this assignment again, how might you do it differently?*

Taken together, these ideas will help you and your students start to think about how you might productively engage with uncertainty. A persistent theme discussed in this book is the idea that we cannot expect our students to be willing to take beautiful risks if we are not willing to do so ourselves.

By modeling a willingness to engage with uncertainty, you will be supporting this type of risk taking in your classroom.

## SUMMARIZING PRINCIPLE

*If* **you want to support creative expression in your classroom,** *then* **you and your students need to have courage and confidence to respond creatively to uncertainty.**

This involves being able to distinguish between different types of uncertainty, establish a supportive and structured learning environment, the willingness to engage with uncertainty that emerges in your teaching, and incorporate frequent opportunities for your students to engage with uncertainty in the learning experiences you design.

Taking the beautiful risk of welcoming uncertainty in your classroom can pay off in the form of developing your students' confidence and competence in responding more creatively to uncertainty in and outside of the classroom.

*Chapter Four*

# The Beautiful Risk of Going Off Script

Don't play what's there, play what's not there.

—Miles Davis

Teaching is an intentional activity. We teach with a goal in mind (Hirst, 1971). Regardless of how streamlined or informal a lesson plan, we typically have some sense of direction or script in mind whenever we engage in the act of teaching. As discussed in chapter 3, we find comfort and direction in having a plan.

Researchers who have looked at reasons why teachers engage in lesson planning have found that one of the most common reasons is to establish a sense of direction, confidence, and security in their lessons (Clark, 1983). Planning helps to eliminate the psychological discomfort that might otherwise be felt when attempting to teach a lesson with no established plan.

Teaching without a general plan or sense of direction can quickly start to feel like an impending instructional train wreck. Many early career teachers quickly come to realize the comfort afforded by an over planned lesson as compared to "running out of material" from a poorly planned lesson (Galluzzo & Kacer, 1991).

It is therefore not surprising that even when a lesson starts to go sideways, we find ourselves gripping even more tightly to the plan (rather than setting it down). Classroom researchers have long noted that making midstream changes during a lesson is difficult. Clark and Yinger (1977), for instance, have explained "teachers tend not to change the instructional process in midstream, even when it is going poorly" (Clark & Yinger, 1977, p. 301).

Sticking to the script is therefore a favored option of both practicing and prospective teachers (Beghetto, 2013; Kennedy, 2005). As noted in chapter

35

3, however, there are times when it is more beneficial to go off script rather than stick to it. The purpose of this chapter is to discuss when it is (and is not) beneficial to go off script. Opportunities and barriers for doing so are also discussed.

## HOW GOING OFF SCRIPT CAN SUPPORT CREATIVITY

Accomplished creators anticipate, recognize, and capitalize on the creative possibilities afforded by going off script. When they hit a wrong note or face unexpected moments in the midst of their professional work, they have the confidence and courage to move away from the routine and toward the unexpected (Beghetto, 2013).

This is because accomplished creators have fine-tuned their awareness to be able to recognize and then act on subtle differences in their routine work. The willingness to notice and engage with the unexpected seems to be a shared characteristic of all accomplished creators who are able to think and act in new ways.

Consider, for instance, Francis Darwin's description of the mindset that led to the discoveries of his father, Charles Darwin:

> A few of his mental characteristics, bearing especially on his mode of working, occur to me. There was one quality of mind which seemed to be of special and extreme advantage in leading him to make discoveries. *It was the power of never letting exceptions pass unnoticed.*
>
> Everybody notices a fact as an exception when it is striking or frequent, but he had a special instinct for arresting an exception . . . In a certain sense there is nothing special in this procedure, many discoveries being made by means of it (Darwin, 1888, pp. 148–149, italics added)

As Darwin's son notes, many other accomplished creators seem to share this approach. Successful improvisers—be they in jazz, on the stage, in front of the classroom, or in life—take up a wrong note in such a way as to say "yes" to it (Henry, 2017). Miles Davis, the American jazz great, put it beautifully, "If you hit a wrong note, it's the next you play that determines whether it is good or bad."

In the documentary film *Possibilities,* Herbie Hancock, who played jazz with Miles Davis, described learning from Davis that "jazz is of the moment. You play the moment" (Biro & Fine, 2006). Hancock explained that approaching this kind of uncertainty is not an easy thing to do; it takes a lot courage, a lot of trust, and a willingness to be vulnerable.

Hancock further explained that Miles provided an opportunity for the young members of his band to move away from scripted performances and, instead, examine the uncertainty of the moment, reach beyond their comfort zone, and create something new by going into areas where they "didn't know intellectually or musically what the end result would be" (Biro & Fine, 2006).

As I've discussed elsewhere (Beghetto, 2013), Claude Monet, the impressionist painter, represents one of the best examples of this approach. Monet devoted long stretches of time focused on the subtle changes and unexpected features that played out in a seemingly static setting (Stokes, 2001). He would sit in a boat for hours, focusing on a particular object and produce various paintings across different times of day and varying weather conditions.

Monet had an eye for "the visual freshness of that first fleeting moment, free of categories of perception or traditional precept" (Heinrich, 2000, p. 32). Consequently, he was able to anticipate and realize the creative potential of seemingly mundane scenes.

Monet had such an eye for the subtleties of the unexpected that Paul Cezanne, described Monet by saying, "He was only an eye—but what an eye!" (cited in Heinrich, 2000, p. 32). What if you and your students approached the moments that emerge in your classroom with the mindset of Darwin, the courage of Miles Davis, or the eye of Monet?

At first blush it may seem unrealistic to compare the process of realizing the creative potential of surprising classroom moments with that of legendary creators. Recall, however, what Darwin's son noted, "there is nothing special in this procedure" (Darwin, 1888, p. 149). Creative discoveries—including those in your own classroom—can result from actively noticing and acting on the creative openings that emerge in your everyday lessons.

## Taking the Beautiful Risk

As discussed in the previous section, taking the beautiful risk of going off script is about recognizing and exploring a surprising turn of events. In the context of the classroom, this does not mean that you should toss your lesson plan out the window or encourage your students to disregard your rules, procedures, or guidelines. Rather, it is about being sensitive to surprising moments and being willing to briefly explore them.

After briefly exploring a particular moment, you may decide that it is not worth pursuing any further because it will lead to a curricular dead-end, create confusion, or take up too much class time. The key is being willing to explore such moments in the first place. This is because it is difficult (if not impossible) to predict in advance whether pursuing a curricular opening will lead to a beneficial outcome (Beghetto, 2016c).

In some cases, going off script will result in creative outcomes. In other cases, it will not. Pursuing a particular opening does not guarantee a creative outcome. But failing to notice and explore such openings will guarantee that you miss the creative openings when they are present.

Although you may not be able to predict whether going off script will result in a creative outcome, you can take steps to help ensure the likelihood of such outcomes (and minimize the potential hazards). One of the first steps is to consider what constitutes a beneficial outcome of going off script.

Building on the basic criteria introduced in chapter 2, a creative outcome resulting from going off script refers to something that represents new insights, perspectives, connections, and ways of thinking (or acting) *and* still connects to pre established learning goals, criteria, and objectives.

Simply stated, a creative outcome meets the criteria in a different way than what you expected. Classroom discussions serve as promising vehicles for opportunities for creative outcomes (Beghetto, 2013). This is because whenever we invite student responses, we have the potential to hear unexpected ideas and points of view.

As long as we are willing to productively go off script and improvise with these moments (Sawyer, 2004), then we can realize the creative potential of these moments. One way of thinking about going off script is that it is made up of the "Rs" of creative openings: *curricular rupture, curricular responses,* and *curricular result* (Beghetto, 2016c). The following sections discuss each of these three phases.

## Noticing Curricular Ruptures

As discussed, no matter how carefully we plan a learning activity, there will always be surprising moments. One reason is because we are not clairvoyant. We can't anticipate everything that will happen in a lesson or activity. Another reason is classrooms are dynamic social spaces, which always have some level of unpredictability (Doyle, 1996).

Sometimes the surprising moments we encounter in our lessons are barely noticeable (e.g., your students are distracted or disengaged during an activity that usually holds their interest). Other times these moments stop us in our instructional tracks (e.g., the technology we were using stops working and we have no backup plan).

Either way, these ruptures open a window of creative possibility that can lead to new ways of thinking and acting. In order to realize the creative potential that these openings afford to us, we need to prepare ourselves for them. Doing so is easier said than done. There are two key hazards that can prevent us from seeing and acting on these possibilities, which are discussed below.

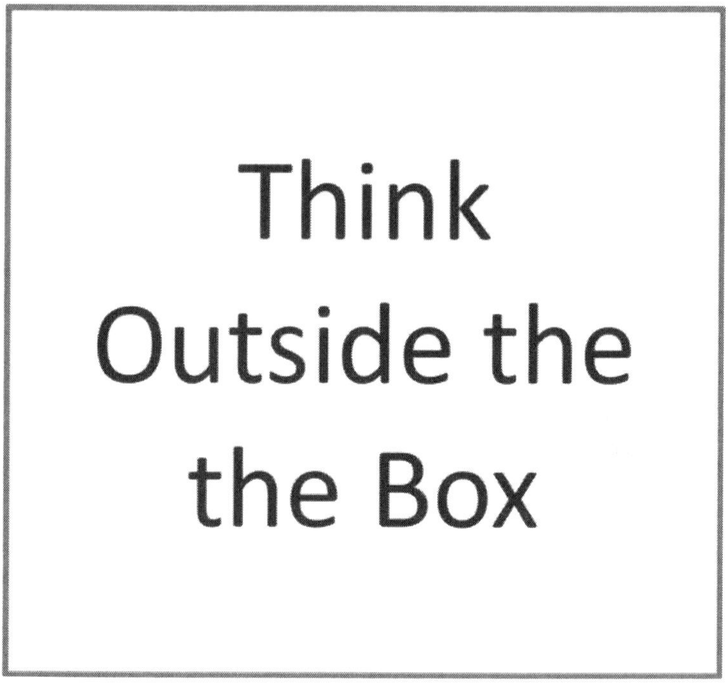

# Think Outside the the Box

Figure 4.1.   Blinded by the Unexpected?

**The Hazard of Being Blinded by the Unexpected.** Take a quick look at figure 4.1. What do you see? Do you see a square with the words, "*Think Outside the Box*" written in the center? If so, you are not alone. Many people see the same thing.

Perhaps you see something different. Take another look. If you look closely you will see the text actually reads, "*Think Outside **the the** Box.*" If you missed the extra "the" it is likely because you are aware of the well-known phrase "Think Outside the Box."

One way psychologists have explained why people fail to see things like the extra "the" in figure 4.1, is because we are influenced by our prior experiences (Eysenck & Keane, 2013) and therefore expected that the phrase has only one "the" not two. If you noticed the extra "the" the first time, you may be aware of similar perceptual tricks (e.g., "Paris in the the Spring") based on prior experience or you paid extra attention to what was written in the box.

The point is that we sometimes fail to notice even the most surprising of events. Researchers have conducted various studies demonstrating that some portion of us tends to miss unexpected events (e.g., dancing gorillas, a woman with an open umbrella) that briefly appear in a video clip of people doing other things (e.g., a small circle of people passing a ball to each other).

Psychologists call this *inattentional blindness* (Mack & Rock, 1998), and it occurs when people are focusing their attention on some feature of the situation other than the unexpected event. In the context of your classroom, these unexpected events can appear in various forms.

A student who rarely raises her hand decides to raise her hand today because she has a particularly unique insight to share. Unfortunately, her willingness to participate goes unnoticed because we are too focused on the students who always raise their hands. One way to avoid this hazard is to actively look for the unexpected (i.e., expect the unexpected).

By doing so, you'll be more likely to recognize these moments when they occur. In addition to expecting and recognizing these emergent opportunities when they appear in your classroom, it is also important to maintain an active awareness of the various possibilities that are always present in any lesson or activity.

**The Hazard of Disappearing Possibilities.** When we become so focused on attaining the goals of a lesson, other creative possibilities tend to disappear right before our eyes. Figure 4.2 provides a helpful visual reminder of this tendency.

Look at figure 4.2 and imagine the small black dot in the middle of this figure is an instructional objective you are trying to attain. Imagine that the larger dots surrounding the small black dot are curricular possibilities. Now focus only on the small black dot (the instructional objective). What happens to the curricular possibilities?

If you look long enough at the small black dot, the surrounding curricular possibilities will literally disappear before your eyes. This has been called *Troxler fading*, named after the Swiss physician Ignaz Paul Vital Troxler. Troxler (1804) found that when we stare intensely at some portion of our visual field, it can cause stationary features in our surrounding environment to fade from our visual perception.

For our purposes, it can serve as a helpful reminder of the hazards involved in becoming too focused on getting to the next learning objective of the lesson, the next slide in the PowerPoint presentation, or the next activity we have planned. Indeed, if we are so focused on moving forward, then we will miss out on the curricular openings that are available to us.

It is therefore important that we focus on *being here* in the moment of our lesson rather than focusing so much on *getting there* to the next learning objective. At this point, an example of the benefits of recognizing and exploring such openings may be helpful. Let's consider a seemingly mundane moment of apparent confusion that occurred in a routine fifth grade math lesson (described in Lampert, Rittenhouse, & Crumbaugh, 1996; Sawyer, 2004).

**Figure 4.2.  Disappearing Possibilities?**
Note. This image was created by the author and adapted from a similar image retrieved from https://illutioni
sta.blogspot.com/2011/03/disappearing-color-spots-illusion_26.html.

The class was discussing what rule they might come up with for explaining how to get from 8 to 4, 4 to 2, 2 to 1, and 0 to 0. One student, Ellie, explained that there were "a whole bunch of rules you could use . . . divide by two— And you could do, um, minus one-half" (Lampert et al., 1996, p. 732). The expected "rule" here would be divide by two, which Ellie mentions. But Ellie also mentioned that you could "minus one-half."

This statement represented an unexpected moment and the teacher explored it by asking Ellie, "And eight minus a half is?" Ellie responded "Four" and her response was met with a "gasp" from her peers, and several students attempted to enter the conversation at this point (Lampert et al., 1996, p. 733).

Ellie's claim that eight minus a half equals four was surprising and seemed like a clear mistake to her peers. Ellie's unexpected idea is an example of a rupture, which warrants a further response from the teacher. If you were the teacher, how would you respond?

You might feel caught between *either* ensuring that students develop a mathematically accurate understanding *or* exploring the student's assertion. Both choices contain hazards and benefits. Correcting the student has the benefit of helping to ensure a mathematically accurate understanding but risks missing out on a potentially generative discussion of this student's thinking.

Going off script and exploring the student's surprising comment may lead to new insights, but it also runs the risk of causing confusion and taking extra class time. Let's consider how to take the beautiful risk of going off script to respond to curricular moments such as this one—addressing the potential hazards and trying to maximize the potential benefits.

## *Responding to Curricular Ruptures*

Once you experience an unexpected opening, the next step is to decide how to respond. As mentioned, you may feel caught between wanting to pursue your pre established curricular goals and going off script to explore new possibilities. The beautiful risk, in this case, requires taking a *both/and* rather than *either/or* approach (Beghetto, 2010).

Creatively teaching your way through such moments involves exploring whether and how you can simultaneously support student learning *and* provide opportunities for students to clarify their thinking. Indeed, keeping *both* in our field of vision we can move between the central academic goal *and* still explore possibilities related to that goal. As with noticing openings, responding to unexpected possibilities requires an active awareness and willingness to step into the uncertainty of those openings.

Doing so requires trusting ourselves and our students to strike a balance between planned and unexpected aspects of the lesson. Look back at the image in figure 4.2. You can use it as a visual reminder of how you can attain this balance by active awareness.

When you actively move your gaze around the image displayed in figure 4.2, you are able to keep your academic goal in focus (i.e., the small black dot), while still quickly exploring each possibility (larger dot). This visual reminder highlights the importance of at least briefly exploring new possibilities as they emerge, while still keeping your learning goals in mind.

Let's return to the fifth grade math example. Recall that Ellie asserted: eight minus a half equals four. Her peers were aghast by this comment and were ready to jump into the conversation and correct her. Her teacher had several options in this moment. One option would be to directly correct Ellie and try to get the lesson back on track, saying something like,

> I agree with your rule of dividing by two, but not minus a half. Eight minus a half is not four. Let's stick with the divide by two rule and see if it works with the other number pairs we have.

Another option would be to invite the other students into the conversation and perhaps even have them provide correction. Yet another option would be to explore this further with Ellie, holding the other students who want to join in at bay. There are various other options. What would you do? How might you take the beautiful risk of going off script, while still maintaining a connection to your immediate and broader learning goals?

Let's consider what the teacher did. The teacher first decided that she would use this moment to connect to some broader mathematical learning goals for Ellie and the students in the class. The teacher recognized that she could use this opportunity to have students engage in mathematical discourse but would first need to establish some guidelines and expectations to productively guide the discussion (Lampert et al., 1999).

More specifically, she wanted to provide Ellie with an opportunity to "practice mathematics" by explaining her thinking. She established ground rules that:

- allowed students to enter the conversation,
- provided opportunities for them to express points of view that differed from Ellie's,
- required them to express their thinking using mathematical symbols,
- encouraged them to try to understand each other,
- supported them in trying to arrive at shared understanding, and
- required them to take Ellie's seemingly incorrect ideas *seriously* and treating Ellie's and each other's ideas *with respect* (Lampert et al., 1996).

Ellie's teacher made this decision on the fly. But she didn't simply leap blindly off script. She first established ground rules and expectations for how the class would take the beautiful risk of going off script. This is an instructive example of how an experienced teacher can, in the moment, establish a way to help minimize potential hazards and maximize potential benefits of taking this kind of beautiful risk.

Productively going off script requires preparing your students and yourself for moving into this new direction guided by broader learning goals. Doing so may involve reminding students (and yourself) of the guidelines and even intervening in the moment to support what may be new patterns of interaction for your classroom.

Establishing new patterns of interaction is particularly helpful when going off script during whole-group discussions. Indeed, your students likely have become accustomed to typical patterns of classroom talk (Black & Wiliam, 1998; Cazden, 2001; Mehan, 1979), which are more like a game of *intellectual hide-and-seek* (Beghetto, 2013) than a genuine exploration of ideas.

Indeed, the typical pattern of whole-class discussion tends to involve a rapidly repeating sequence. It starts with the teacher asking a question with a predetermined answer. Then students who think they know the answer vie for a chance to provide the expected response. Next, the teacher quickly evaluates whether the response matches what was expected, and the process starts again. (Beghetto, 2013).

Taking the beautiful risk of going off script requires moving away from typical patterns of classroom discussion, which are guided by a somewhat closed and predetermined curricular outcome. And, instead, moving into a more open and emergent exploration of ideas, which can lead to different and potentially creative learning outcomes.

## Anticipating and Evaluating Curricular Results

As discussed, creativity is emergent. There are no guarantees that going off script will actually lead to creative outcomes. That said, there are some things you can do to help increase the chances of supporting a positive outcome.

The key is to do your best to consider benefits and hazards, trust your professional judgment, and take the action that you feel will be the most likely to maximize a creative learning outcome for your students. The teacher from the Ellie example discussed above provides an excellent model of this kind of "in-the-moment" thinking and action.

By taking a few moments to quickly establish simple guidelines and expectations as you go off script together, you and your students will be in a position to evaluate the results of your actions, which can guide subsequent choices and actions. In the case of Ellie's teacher, the guidelines enabled the class to move into a generative mathematical discussion of important assumptions, definitions, and nuances in Ellie's claim that "eight minus one-half is four" (Lampert et al., 1996).

Specifically, students were able to explore the connection Ellie was attempting to articulate: one-half being a *quantity* (one-half of a whole, half of eight is four). And how this connection was in contrast to the way other students were viewing one-half as being an *operator on quantities* (e.g., 8 - .5 = 7.5), which resulted in the disagreement.

In addition to learning how to engage in mathematical discourse about a somewhat complex distinction, they also learned how to disagree respectfully, share tentative or "first draft" ideas, express evidence, and revise their thinking and understanding together (Lampert et al., 1996, pp. 734–737).

Of course, going off script will not always turn out like the Ellie example. No matter what the outcome, you and your students can still learn from these experiences and establish a different approach for addressing similar situations in the future. Conversely, if your response was beneficial, you can develop your courage and confidence to make similar decisions.

Ultimately you have two basic options whenever you experience a curricular opening in your teaching: *sticking with the plan* or *going off script.*

In some cases, the best option will be to stick with the plan. In other cases, it will be more beneficial to take the beautiful risk of going off script. At this point, it may be helpful to quickly consider both options and how you might anticipate and evaluate the results of each.

**Sticking to the Plan.** The first option we have when confronted with an unexpected moment is to simply stick with the plan.

*Anticipating the results.* The clear benefit of this option is that we can move forward with the lesson as planned. There are, however, hazards involved. If moving forward involves dismissing or correcting ideas, even if done so gently (e.g., "Why don't you think about that some more and I'll call on someone else"), then we can miss opportunities to explore potentially generative new directions (recall the example of Ellie).

*Evaluating the results.* Although our primary aim when dismissing or redirecting a student idea is to continue on with the planned lesson, doing so can also discourage our students' willingness to share their unique ideas, perspectives, and questions (Beghetto, 2013). Even in cases where students may be confused, we miss opportunities to provide further clarification, which may benefit the understanding of multiple students.

There are, of course, situations when gentle redirecting a student's unexpected response are appropriate and necessary (e.g., we do not have enough time to address an idea given other planned activities). In such cases, it is important to redirect in a way that students still feel heard and supported in sharing their ideas.

Simple strategies like those discussed in chapter 3 (e.g., designating a corner of the chalkboard for "wonder wall") can ensure that students recognize that although there may not be time to address a question or idea at this particular moment, their perspectives are still welcome and will be addressed at a later time.

In sum, sticking to the plan is sometimes necessary but there are various hazards involved. These hazards can make sticking to the plan a bad risk because of the potential unanticipated harm it can do to the overall climate of the classroom and students' willingness to share their ideas (Beghetto, 2013).

When used sparingly and with a commitment to revisit ideas that students have, it is a viable option. In most cases, however, it is worth the effort to take the beautiful risk to go off script—even if momentarily—to briefly explore new possibilities.

**Going off script.** Going off script requires taking a moment to at least briefly explore an unexpected opening. As mentioned, going off script does not mean entirely abandoning the lesson. It also doesn't mean you'll never return to the planned lesson. But it does, at a minimum, require taking a temporary detour.

*Anticipating the results.* Going off script (even briefly) involves potential hazards. Indeed, taking time to explore a surprising question or perspective can take the lesson offtrack, use up precious instructional time, and even cause confusion amongst other students. These are legitimate concerns that many teachers have when faced with the possibility of going off script (Kennedy, 2005).

This hazard, however, can be mitigated if we establish some simple guidelines, even saying something as simple as "Let's take a moment and explore this idea and then we'll decide whether to return to the lesson or pursue it a bit more." After taking a moment to explore the idea or opening, you can then decide on the next step.

You may quickly determine that this new direction should be shelved and returned to later. Alternatively, you may decide that the new direction has potential and warrants further exploration, even if it takes the discussion or lesson in an emergent direction.

*Evaluating the results.* Even seemingly mistaken or incorrect student conceptions can support student understanding. As illustrated in the Ellie example, addressing what seems like an incorrect response can help all students develop a more precise academic understanding of key concepts, definitions, and distinctions.

It can also develop productive norms of classroom participation and patterns of discourse. Without exploring unexpected ideas, even briefly, opportunities for individual clarification and potential contributions to the learning of others are lost.

Consequently, going off script—while still keeping an eye toward your overall instructional goals—represents a beautiful risk, which can result in the attainment of various learning goals. Indeed, in addition to meeting immediate learning goals, going off script can enable your students to attain other important (and even unanticipated) learning goals.

These goals include:

- clarifying their understanding;
- supporting their confidence; and
- providing them with an opportunity to share their mini-c ideas and make little-c contributions to the learning and understanding of others.

## SUMMARIZING ACTION PRINCIPLE

*If* you want to support creative expression in your classroom, *then* you need to have courage and confidence to decide when it is (and is not) beneficial to go off script.

Productively going off script involves an active willingness to *notice* curricular openings, *respond* to those openings, and evaluate the *results* of your response. Taking the beautiful risk of going off script will help you establish a classroom environment that welcomes and supports unique student perspectives.

The key is recognizing that there is more to supporting creative expression than simple verbal encouragement (e.g., "All ideas are welcome"). When it comes to supporting creative expression in the classroom, it is more about how we actually respond to unexpected ideas that determines whether students' creative expression will be supported or suppressed.

Unexpected moments serve as defining moments (Beghetto, 2013). They define who we are as teachers for our students and for ourselves. Our responses in these moments clearly communicate to our students whether what we say is important is actually demonstrated in our actions. They define for our students whether they can *actually* trust us with their emerging ideas, perspectives, and questions—or not.

*Chapter Five*

# The Beautiful Risk of Planning Creative Openings

The difficulty lies not so much in developing new ideas as in escaping from old ones.

—John Maynard Keynes

Creativity can come from surprising moments in your curriculum. These moments can emerge unexpectedly (as discussed in chapter 4) or you can *plan* openings in your curriculum to provide opportunities for your students to creatively engage with uncertainty.

When uncertainty emerges from an unexpected turn in your curriculum (e.g., a student shares a surprising insight), the goal is to know how to support students' creative expression by knowing when and how to take the beautiful risk of going off script. The focus of this chapter, however, is knowing how to take the beautiful risk of intentionally opening up your curriculum for creative expression.

## MAKING ROOM FOR CREATIVITY

Our students typically are asked to complete activities and assignments in which most everything is determined in advance (Beghetto, 2018):

- *what they are being asked to do,*
- *how they are being asked to do it,*
- *the resulting product, and*
- *the criteria for success.*

When everything is predetermined, there is not much room for creative expression. This is because students are rewarded for providing expected responses, not unexpected ones. This is not to say that predetermined learning exercises have no value. Students can and do benefit from them—particularly when they are initially introduced to a concept or skill.

If students have not developed a basic understanding of the concepts and principles they need to learn, then requiring them to come up with their own problems or ways of solving problems can be disadvantageous. The result will be "unnecessary excessive floundering" (Lee & Anderson, 2012, p. 462), not creativity.

A better way to think about overdesigned assignments is that they represent an initially necessary, albeit temporary, step toward creative learning. They're like academic training wheels, because they serve to eliminate most of the uncertainty about the task by providing extra support.

Overdesigned activities and assignments thereby provide students with temporary supports that enable them to practice what they have been taught. This will prepare them to take the next step of putting their understanding of what they have been taught to creative use. Figure 5.1 provides a visual illustration of an overdesigned learning activity.

As illustrated in figure 5.1, over designed assignments provide students with a solid structure that surrounds them with clear expectations about what they are expected to do, how they are expected to do it, what the result should be, and the criteria for determining a successful outcome (Beghetto, 2018).

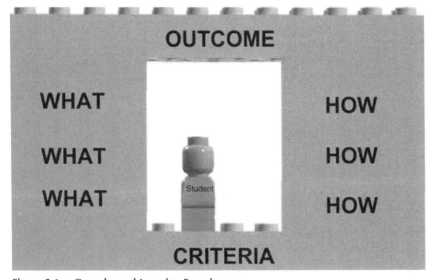

**Figure 5.1.   Overplanned Learning Experiences**
Note: Image designed by author LEGO® Digital Designer freeware was used to model the bricks and figurine.

As mentioned, this type of learning experience can help students develop and reinforce their understanding of a topic, skill, or concept that has been recently taught to them. Here's a quick example.

Consider a middle school social studies teacher who has taught a lesson on how to use the coordinates of a map to find locations in Southeast Asia. Immediately after teaching the lesson, the teacher provides students with a worksheet that includes a detailed map of Southeast Asia, five different sets of coordinates, and five blanks to write the physical locations associated with the coordinates.

Students are then instructed to independently complete the worksheet to help reinforce what was just taught. In this example all of the aspects of this learning task have been predetermined by the teacher. Using this activity makes sense if the goal is to reinforce and quickly check students' understanding of a previously taught skill or concept.

The key benefit of this exercise is that there is not much ambiguity in what students are being asked to do. In this way, over designed learning assignments are not, in themselves, a bad thing. They only become problematic if they represent the predominate or only type of experience we provide for our students.

Given that students are boxed in with predetermined expectations, they have little or no room for creative expression. This is because, as Stokes (2010) has explained, "creativity is only possible with incompletely defined, ill-structured problems" (p. 91). The good news about over planned learning activities is that they are already halfway to becoming a creative activity.

Recall from chapter 2, classroom creativity is about finding new ways of meeting the criteria of a task, activity, or assignment. Over planned activities and assignments have plenty of constraints; all that is needed is an opening for original expression.

## Small Openings

If overdesigned exercises are like training wheels, then we need to provide activities that allow students to remove those training wheels and put their learning to creative use. Just like training wheels, you can start small. Indeed, removing just one of the wheels helps someone learning to ride a bike develop his or her balance and confidence. The same can be said about opening up over planned assignments.

Even small openings can lead to creative possibilities. Using the process of *lesson unplanning* (Beghetto, 2017b, 2018), you can transform any overdesigned learning tasks into a creative learning experience. Lesson unplanning involves removing one or more predetermined features of an activity or assignment to make room for creative expression.[1]

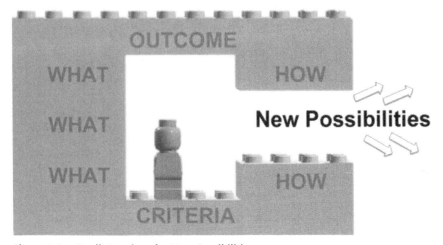

**Figure 5.2. Small Openings for New Possibilities**
Note: Image designed by author LEGO® Digital Designer freeware was used to model the bricks and
figurine.

Figure 5.2 provides a visual illustration of this process.

As depicted in figure 5.2, if we remove even one predetermined feature of a task, we establish openings for new possibilities to emerge.

Let's quickly return to the social studies example and see how this might apply. After having students use the worksheet to demonstrate that they can identify several predetermined physical features on a map of Southeast Asia, the teacher can then open up the lesson and invite students to come up with their own problems, such as providing the coordinates from any geographic region of their choosing.

The teacher can open up the activity even further by having students make up their own maps and coordinate systems for locating specific features of imaginary lands that they have read about (e.g., Hogwarts, Narnia) or created themselves (e.g., a map of a virtual world they created in one of their favorite video games).

Lesson unplanning can be applied to any subject or topic, including subjects that may initially seem somewhat fixed and closed (see Beghetto, 2018). Consider math, for example. You might start by demonstrating one way of solving a particular type of problem and then ask students to come up with as many ways of solving the problem as they can.

This differs from the typical approach of teaching one procedure for solving a problem and then assigning several practice problems which can be solved in that same way. Instead, the class has the opportunity to solve one problem multiple ways. If the class comes up with ten unique and mathematically accurate ways of solving a problem, then a student who knows two ways of solving a problem will get to see eight additional ways.

Even the teacher may discover a few new ways of solving the problem. Of course, if a student is not capable of understanding even one way of solving the problem, then sharing ten or more ways can actually result in additional confusion or frustration. Students therefore need to be ready to take on the added challenge that lesson unplanning provides. Indeed, as Lee and Anderson (2013) have explained,

> When students do not have enough prior knowledge, two simultaneously presented worked examples are simply two unfamiliar examples. (p. 459)

With this in mind, it is important to recognize that some of your students will need additional practice prior to taking on more challenging learning experiences, whereas other students will be ready for even more complex challenges (Beghetto, 2018).

## Pushing Out the Walls and Removing the Ceiling

Taking the beautiful risk of establishing creative openings in your classroom also involves providing young people (and yourself) with opportunities to engage with and address real-world problems. Tackling real-world problems expands student learning beyond the classroom and enables students to make creative contributions to others.

Figure 5.3 provides a visual representation of these type of openings.

As illustrated in figure 5.3, you can push out the walls and remove the ceiling on creative learning experiences by designing challenges that establish openings in what students do, how they do it, and the resulting outcome. In such cases, the problems, processes, and products are to-be-determined by students, but with your support.

These are not free-range experiences that occur without any guidance, structure, or support. As illustrated in figure 5.3, there is still a well-defined and supportive structure of criteria that students stand on, which includes clear directions and assistance for students as they work to define what they will be doing, how they will be doing it, and the resulting outcome.

In this way, such experiences provide a great deal of agency for students, while at the same time providing clear criteria, guidelines, and as-needed instructional support. With these supports in place, your students can take on the challenge of creatively engaging with uncertainty, within predetermined limits and criteria that you (and your students) establish.

Challenging students to tackle problems that they identify as important is one of the most promising vehicles for helping students develop their

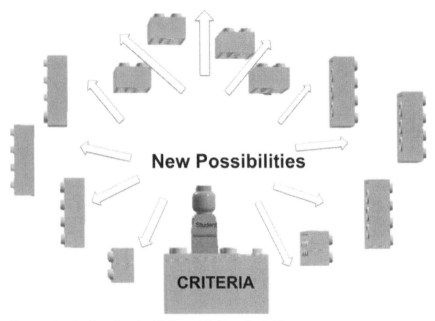

**Figure 5.3.   Pushing Out the Walls and Raising the Ceilings**
Note: Image designed by author LEGO® Digital Designer freeware was used to model the bricks and
  figurine.

confidence, awareness, and understanding of how to put their learning to creative use. An example of this type of learning experience is called a *legacy
challenge* (for a detailed overview, see Beghetto, 2018).

Legacy challenges provide students with opportunities to respond to uncertainty in a way that makes a creative contribution in and outside their
classroom. Here's an example:

**Students identify a problem they care about**. A group of seventh grade
  students recognize there are children and families they know who need
  warm winter clothing, but can't afford it;
**Students develop and communicate an argument about why the prob-
  lem matters to others and needs to be addressed**. Students engage in
  research to identify the scope of the problem, who is most impacted by the
  problem, and how they might increase awareness about the problem;
**Students develop a plan to do something about the problem**. Students
  partner with outside experts and community organizations to establish a
  discreet and efficient way of providing winter clothing to children and
  families in need; and

**Students develop a plan to help ensure their work will carry on.** Students establish a legacy plan for their work with outside organizations and incoming seventh graders interested in the project who will carry the work forward each year.

When provided with the opportunity, students can use a vehicle like legacy challenges to make the walls of the classroom permeable, establish creative openings for community members to be involved in student work, and to help students make ongoing contributions to the external community.

Legacy challenges serve to flip the typical academic model. Whereas a typical academic project or activity is designed to teach a particular skill or concept, legacy challenges provide a vehicle for creatively using academic learning to develop sustainable solutions to problems that students identify in their schools, communities, and the broader community (Beghetto, 2018).

## HOW TO TAKE THE BEAUTIFUL RISK

Supporting creative expression in your classroom requires opening up your lessons and activities. By making openings in your learning activities, even small ones, your students will have an opportunity to develop their creative confidence and competence by learning how to meet predefined criteria in their own unique way.

As with all beautiful risks, there are some hazards to acknowledge and address so that you can increase the benefits of establishing openings in your curriculum.

### Start with What You Have

Taking the beautiful risk of making creative openings in your curriculum requires a bit of planning or, more accurately, a bit of unplanning. A potential hazard of taking this risk is believing that you need to start from scratch and finding yourself overwhelmed by the idea of developing an entirely new set of learning activities and experiences.

The good news is you do not need to design activities from scratch. Rather, you can start with existing activities and assignments and transform them by replacing some predetermined aspect with a to-be-determined component. Each time you teach a particular topic, take a moment to think through various learning activities and assignments you have designed for that topic.

Then consider how you might open up some of the features of those existing tasks to allow students to come up with their own way of meeting the criteria you have defined. You can still use your existing activity but compliment it with some activities that provide students with additional options for what they do, how they do it, and what the result might look like (see Beghetto, 2018, for a detailed account of this process).

In this way, creative learning tasks are a shared responsibility. You, as the teacher, have the responsibility of establishing and clarifying the criteria of any specific task and your students are responsible for meeting the criteria with your support. Here's a simple formula to help you and your students remember this:

*Clarify the Criteria [you]* **x** *Different Ways to Meet the Criteria [your students + you]* = ***Creative Learning Outcomes***

Each component is briefly discussed in the sections that follow.

**Clarifying the Criteria.** The first part of this shared responsibility is for you to clarify the criteria.

- *What's the point of this task?*
- *What do I hope my students will get out of this experience?*
- *What do students need to demonstrate to be successful?*
- *What time and material constraints do we need to operate within?*

Let's consider a sixth grade science teacher who uses a video and worksheet to help reinforce her students' understanding of evolutionary adaptations. After teaching the concepts, the teacher asks students to watch a brief video of five different plant adaptations on their tablets.

She provides a worksheet that requires students to list the plant names presented in the video, an adaption, and to briefly explain the benefit. All of the information necessary for completing this worksheet is in the video. If her goal is to reinforce and creatively expand students' understanding of evolutionary adaptions, then the teacher needs to open up possibilities for how students meet the criteria.

One option would be to have students use part of the preexisting activity (e.g., identify three plant adaptions from the first part of the video) and then open up part of the activity so they can generate a few of their own examples (e.g., come up with two adaptions of other plants or an organism). There are countless variations in how this can be accomplished. The key is to provide multiple ways for students to meet the preset criteria.

**Multiple Ways to Meet the Criteria.** Once you clarify the criteria, you can start imagining how to open up alternative ways for your students to meet the criteria you have established. Another way of thinking about designing this type of creative learning activity is for you to decide the "must-haves" and then provide multiple ways for students to meet those must-haves.

By changing how we think about learning activities, we can start to realize that our students can be given a lot more room to creatively work within required academic constraints and criteria. Once you develop your confidence opening up existing lessons, you'll be ready to design and use more creative curricula in your classroom (see also chapter 8).

## Making Just-in-Time Adjustments

In addition to clarifying criteria and providing multiple ways for students to meet those criteria, taking the beautiful risk of making creative openings requires flexibility in how you provide creative opportunities and supports.

Although planning for openings in your curriculum is a good way to ensure that students have an opportunity to creatively meet expectations, you also need to be ready to respond in the moment to the emerging needs of your students.

As mentioned, some of your students will need more instructional support before they are ready to come up with their own way of meeting the criteria of a creative learning task you have designed. It is therefore a good idea to be ready to have a few examples or options available for students who might need them.

An example of this might be an activity where you introduce the components of a research project and then ask students to come up with their own topic. Some students may be ready to dive in, whereas others will need some guidance. You can anticipate this by having a list of starter topics and ideas.

When using this additional support, you'll still want to challenge students to come up with something interesting to them that is inspired by the list. By using the list in this way, you can help kick-start the process of students generating their own research topics. The key would be letting them know that the list you are providing is just a starter list and that they are expected to modify one of the example topics or, better yet, come up with their own.

Simple instructional moves like providing a starter list, with the added expectation that some level of novelty is required, are a great way to balance the need to provide support and guidance with the expectation that students still need to come up with their own unique insights, perspectives, and approach to the tasks you design.

The flip side of students who need more support are students who need additional challenges. In such cases, you'll want to provide students with the option of having a bit more flexibility so that those who are ready for a more complex challenge can use that to their advantage (Beghetto, 2018).

An example of this might be an activity where you have taught students one procedure for solving a problem and then have them come up with an alternative way. Some students may be ready to push beyond this by also coming up with their own problems.

You can help prepare yourself and your students for this by letting them know that if they can demonstrate their ability to complete the task you designed, that you invite them to continue pushing forward by designing their own tasks for meeting the criteria.

Because it is difficult to predict the kinds of creative insights and outcomes students are capable of producing, the best way of knowing whether students are ready to take on more complex challenges is to provide them with opportunities to do so (Beghetto, 2018). When this happens, students can surprise us (and themselves) with what they are capable of producing (see Whiteley, 2015, for examples).

Taking the beautiful risk of planning for creative openings in your lessons is a dynamic process that involves providing students with a solid instructional foundation to ensure that they understand and are able to fulfill the criteria of an activity and also know how to obtain additional instructional support when necessary.

## SUMMARIZING ACTION PRINCIPLE

*If* you want to provide your students with opportunities for creative expression, *then* you need to plan for these openings in your curriculum.

Our lesson plans can serve as gatekeepers of creativity. If we don't plan for creativity, then "the tyranny of the lesson plan" (Jeffrey Smith, personal communication, August 16, 2008) can take over and deny opportunities for creative expression. Taking the beautiful risk of planning for creativity involves modifying your existing learning activities by making openings in what you already have planned.

You can get started with a small opening (e.g., showing students one way of meeting the criteria of learning a task and asking them to come up with additional ways). As you become more confident with making openings in your assignments and activities, you and your students can push out the walls of possibility and raise the ceiling on what students are asked to do.

This includes designing learning experiences that make creative contributions to other people in your school and community. Indeed, taking the beautiful risk of planning creative openings in your lessons will also help you design more dynamic and engaging creative learning experiences.

Although you still maintain responsibility for establishing the criteria for these experiences, your students have an opportunity to assume responsibility for how those criteria will be fulfilled.

Taking this beautiful risk can also pay out in providing opportunities for you and your students to develop creative confidence by learning and teaching in new and different ways. Most importantly, you and your students will have an opportunity to make creative contributions to the learning and lives of others.

## NOTE

1.  The ideas presented in this (and the following) sections of this chapter provide a brief introduction and overview for how you can create openings in your curriculum to transform routine tasks into more complex challenges (adapted from ideas presented in Beghetto, 2017b; 2018).

## Chapter Six

# The Beautiful Risk of Establishing Creative Learning Environments

The worst enemy to creativity is self-doubt.

—Sylvia Plath

Consider two students. One is highly confident and jumps at the opportunity to discuss the innovative projects she has developed. In fact, she recently won first prize at your state's Invention Contest. Another student is withdrawn, rarely speaks when asked to share her ideas during class, and struggles to complete assignments and tasks.

What might account for the difference between these two students? Is one "gifted" or more "motivated" than the other? Is one student "at risk" of failure and the other showing "great potential" for future success?

What if I told you that these two students are actually the same student?[1] What this vignette illustrates is our tendency to view distinct behaviors as if they always come from different students. Although individual differences do play a role in different behavior, the environment can play an equally if not more profound role (Barker & Wright, 1971).

In fact, some ecological psychologists have gone as far as to argue that it is the behavior setting (environment) itself that most directly influences a person's behavior, not "the individual personalities (or other individual differences) of the inhabitants" (M. Scott, 2005, p. 298). This is not to say individual differences play no role, but rather that contexts and situations matter. This seems to hold true for creative expression as it does any other behavior.

Taking the beautiful risks necessary for establishing a creative learning environment therefore requires that we establish an environment that supports instead of inadvertently suppresses students' willingness to think and act creatively.

# POTENTIAL IS NOT ENOUGH

Having creative potential and acting on that potential are two different things (Karwowski & Beghetto, 2018). Although a student may have demonstrated creative potential in the past or another setting, it doesn't mean that same student will be willing to take the risks necessary to share creative ideas in a different setting or situation.

Moreover, given that all students have creative potential, it is important to understand what environmental factors may impede (rather than encourage) students' willingness to share their ideas, perspectives, and actions. So, what might influence students' creative expression in your classroom?

One way to think about this is: *Your students' creative behavior is connected to a particular situation and how your students' experience that situation.* Let's imagine there's a student in your class who has a creative way of thinking about a topic you are discussing with the class. During a class discussion you invite all of your students to share their unique perspectives about the topic (e.g., "I'd really like to hear different ways of thinking about this topic!").

Why might a student who otherwise has a unique perspective to offer choose not to do so? You can probably come up with a variety of different reasons. Let's consider two interrelated reasons: self-beliefs and situational factors.

## Self-Beliefs

Self-beliefs play an important role in determining whether a student who is capable of taking creative action will actually choose to do so. Although there are a variety of self-beliefs that come into play when taking creative action, two beliefs are particularly important: creative confidence beliefs and creative value beliefs (Karwowski, Lubda, & Beghetto, in press).

Students who are otherwise capable of performing a creative behavior may choose not to try if they do not have the confidence in their ability to do so *or* if they do not see the value in doing so (Bandura, 1997; Chen, 2016; Karwowski & Beghetto, 2018; Pretz & Nelson, 2017). Let's quickly take a look at these two types of beliefs.

**Creative Confidence Beliefs.** Creative confidence beliefs refer to a person's perceived ability to creatively perform a task (Karwowski et al., in press). Examples of creative confidence in the classroom include your students' belief in their ability to come up with creative ideas, solve problems creatively, or generate creative products.

Creative confidence beliefs can be further differentiated into more general creative ability beliefs (e.g., "I'm good at solving math problems creatively") and more situationally specific beliefs (e.g., "I'm confident I can come up with at least three creative solutions to this particular math problem").

Confidence beliefs tend to vary depending on the task to be performed and the particular situation (Beghetto & Karwowski, 2017). A student who appears to be very creative in both math and science may feel confident only in coming up with creative ways of thinking about math problems and have much lower confidence when it comes to science.

It is therefore important to recognize that our general perceptions of students' creative abilities may not align with students' particular beliefs in their ability to creatively perform tasks in particular situations. Moreover, students' beliefs about their abilities often don't match their actual performance (Kruger & Dunning, 1999; Karwowski et al., in press). Some students may underestimate their abilities, whereas others may overestimate.

One way you can help your students develop a more accurate picture of their creative competence is to have your students monitor and keep track of their confidence beliefs whenever they perform tasks that involve creative expression. Doing so can also help them identify challenges that are more aligned with their current level of performance.

Students who, for instance, continually underestimate their abilities can be supported in recognizing that they are capable of performing at higher levels than they think. Students that overestimate their abilities can also be reminded to try setting challenging but more attainable goals.

The message, for all students, should be that growth comes from knowing your current strengths and limitations (Kaufman & Beghetto, 2013). In this way, students can play to their strengths and work on addressing their limitations. This can only come from having students actively monitor and reflect on their beliefs in relation to their actual performance.

Such monitoring need not be elaborate or time consuming; you can make a quick check-in using Google classroom or a log that has them briefly respond to a few questions immediately before and after a particular task.

Here's an example. Prior to completing a task that requires them to generate their own project idea, you could have them rate their confidence on a scale[2] of 0–100 (0 = not at all confident, 100 = completely confident). When having them rate their confidence, it is a good idea to try to set specific target levels (Bandura, 2006), such as:

*How confident are you that you can come up with . . .*

1. *At least one unique idea?*
2. *At least three unique ideas?*
3. *Five or more unique ideas?*

Then, after students have completed the task, you could ask them to briefly compare and discuss their predictions and their actual performance. You can also include additional questions such as:

- *Did you perform at your predicted level, below your predicted level, or above your predicted level? Explain why you think this happened.*
- *What, if anything, surprised you about your performance?*
- *What kinds of things would have helped you perform at an even higher level?*
- *If you were to do this task again, do you predict you would do the same, better, worse? Explain.*

Depending on the students you teach, you might need to modify these questions so that your students can easily understand what they are being asked (you can even read the questions to your class). When students start monitoring and reflecting on their confidence beliefs in relation to their actual performance, they can start to develop a more accurate picture of their current capabilities and set more realistic challenges for themselves (see also Beghetto, 2018).

Moreover, having students share this information with you will provide you with insights into how you can provide more tailored instructional supports for your students.

**Creative Value Beliefs.** Creative value beliefs are more than simply viewing creativity as something important. Rather, creative value beliefs involve viewing creativity as an important part of your identity (Beghetto & Karwowski, 2017). In this way our creative value beliefs influence whether and how we see ourselves as creative people.

Valuing creativity is important to actual performance. Unless people value creativity, there is little chance they will invest the effort to engage in creative behaviors (Karwowski & Beghetto, 2018). Indeed, creative confidence and valuing creativity work together to help connect the link between creative potential and creative performance.

As mentioned, if your students are capable of performing a task creatively but lack confidence in their ability to do so or do not see the value in doing so, then they are less likely to try to express their creativity on the task (Karwowski & Beghetto, 2018). By providing students with multiple opportunities to creatively respond to learning tasks and reflect on those responses, you can support their creative confidence beliefs and help them recognize the value of creative expression.

Doing so can address one of the most persistent hazards to creative expression highlighted in chapter 2: The belief that only some people are capable of creativity. When students recognize that creative expression is an important part of their (and everyone's) identity, then they are more likely to put forth and sustain the effort necessary for creative expression (Karwowski et al., in press).

Just as it is important to provide opportunities for students to reflect on their creative confidence beliefs, it is also helpful to periodically monitor students' creative value beliefs. Here's an example of the kinds of statements you can use to monitor the way students view and value their own creativity (items and wording adapted from Karwowski et al., 2013):

- *I think I am a creative person.*
- *My creativity is important for who I am.*
- *Being a creative person is important to me.*
- *Creativity is an important part of me.*
- *Creativity is a characteristic that is important to me.*

Given that you are not using these items for research purposes, you can use all or some combination of these items. You can also adapt the wording to make them more accessible for your students. You can use a five-point agreement scale with these items (e.g., 1 = strongly disagree, 5 = strongly agree) or even various emoticons (from sad face to smiley face).

Emoticons can be particularly helpful for younger students or students who would benefit from another option. You might start by having students respond to these items at the beginning of the year or semester and then periodically have them complete these items throughout the year or semester. You can let your students know that although there is no "correct" answer, you expect them to respond honestly.

You can also complement these items with a few quick reflection questions that will help them reflect on how creative contributions can benefit them and others. The following is a sample of reflection questions you can modify and use any time your students have completed a task that affords them an opportunity to be creative:

- *How did hearing different ideas from everyone help you?*
- *How did your ideas help others?*
- *Why do you think it is important for everyone to listen to and share different ideas during class discussions and small group activities?*
- *How does coming up with your own ways of [solving problems, doing things, completing tasks] help you learn?*
- *How might it help others learn?*
- *Why is it important to you to have an opportunity to come up with your own ways of doing things?*

By keeping track of their responses to the above items and questions you can get a sense of how students' creativity beliefs might be developing and changing over time. This information will also help you understand why some of your students are more or less engaged in creative opportunities. You can then make any necessary modifications to the kinds of assignments and experiences you design for your students.

The first step in helping your students develop healthy creative self-beliefs is for you and your students to be aware of these beliefs and actively monitor how they are influenced by various experiences in the classroom. This includes understanding how various situational factors can impact these beliefs. The following section briefly highlights some of these factors.

## Situational Factors

Self-beliefs can be influenced by a variety of situational factors, including various personal and environmental factors (Bandura, 1997). Students' creative confidence to perform a specific task can be highly variable, even for students who tend to personally value creativity and generally have confidence in their creative abilities.

If a student is not feeling well on a particular day or is preoccupied by another issue (e.g., a fight with a close friend), then it is unlikely that the student's confidence to perform a specific task creatively will be as high as usual. Similarly, creatively confident students who are sitting next to students who constantly make fun of them for coming up with "weird ideas" may be less likely to share their thoughts during a class discussion.

Aside from these factors, there are also classroom factors that can suppress students' willingness to think and act creatively. Here are a few questions that will serve as a brief preview to some of the key situational factors that will be discussed in the next section:

- **Are you setting (and resetting) a creativity-supportive tone?** Communicating that you value student creativity and beautiful risk taking in your classroom starts on day one and needs to be continually reinforced and revisited with students throughout your time with them.
- **Are you considering your students' perspective?** The intentions behind the way you teach, the procedures you adopt, and how you see things in your classroom can differ (sometimes quite dramatically) from how your students perceive and experience things.
- **Are your routines, procedures, and classroom displays sending creativity-supportive messages to students?** How do features of your classroom, like displays of student work and data walls, influence your students' willingness to think and act creatively?

Having briefly considered the role that self-beliefs and situational factors play in students' creative behavior, let's now consider how you might take the beautiful risk of establishing a creativity-supportive learning environment.

## HOW TO TAKE THE BEAUTIFUL RISK

As mentioned, when it comes to establishing a classroom environment supportive of creative expression, the key is to be aware of the messages being sent and received by students. This includes being aware of not only what we actually say to students, but also how we say it and what the displays, decorations, routines, and procedures also communicate (Beghetto, 2013).

Although we may design learning activities with the best intentions, our perceptions may not align with our students' experiences. We sometimes need to remind ourselves that our perspective can be very different from our students' perspective. Figure 6.1 is a visual reminder of this. When you first look at figure 6.1, what do you immediately see?

**Figure 6.1.   Shifting Your Perspective**
Note. This image was drawn by the author and adapted from a similar image retrieved from https://www. moillusions.com/the-village-elephant-optical-illusion

There are two scenes in figure 6.1 that can be seen by shifting your perspective. When you first viewed this image, did you see a village scene with huts or an elephant?

Whatever you saw first can be thought of as your "teacher" perspective. By continuing to look at the image you will likely see the other option; this can be thought of as the "student" perspective. You cannot see both images simultaneously, you have to shift your perspective between these images.

The point of this "optical illusion" is to serve as a visual reminder that we sometimes need to shift our perspective away from our initial understanding in order to see and understand what our students are experiencing. The best way to demonstrate your commitment to understanding your students' experience is to invite them continually to share their perspectives about your class—starting on day one.

## Start on Day One

Working to establish a creative learning environment starts before students set foot into your classroom. As you plan your first day with students, it is important to demonstrate your commitment to developing the kind of classroom that is supportive of beautiful risk taking.

Rather than play a game of people bingo or engage in some other "icebreaker" activity, why not start with an activity that helps students realize that your classroom is different? Try something that will emphasize that you expect and will support your students in taking beautiful risks.

Here's an example. My daughter's sixth grade math teacher wanted to replace *"I can't"* thinking with an *"I'll keep trying"* mindset. So, on the first day of class, the math teacher asked students to write out one thing they can't do (it didn't have to be in math). She then rolled out a papier-mâché dinosaur, the mouth of the dinosaur was the opening to a trashcan.

She called it the *Icantasaurus* and asked students to feed their "I can't" statements into its mouth. She and her students then agreed that in this math class, they would replace "I can't" statements with something more positive, like "I'll keep trying" or "I need help." Not only does such an activity have the goal of supporting a "growth mindset" (Dweck, 2006), it can also establish a psychologically supportive environment for taking beautiful risks.

In the case of my daughter, this first day activity made a positive and lasting impression on her. Even when my daughter found herself struggling in the class, she felt supported by this teacher (much more so than some of her other teachers). She attributed her willingness to ask for help and share her tentative ideas in this class to feeling supported by this teacher from day one.

You need not replicate the *Icantasaurus* activity to communicate a similar message. A simple writing prompt that invites your students to share a bit about themselves as students and what you can do to support them can go a long way to communicate that you care about their experiences. And, you likely will be surprised by the honesty and risks students will take when invited to do so.

Here's an example. Joan Cone, a twelfth grade English teacher, asked her students on day one of the class to complete the following assignment:[3]

> Write me a letter telling me about yourself—your history as a student; your family life, social life, work life, extracurricular activities, plans for the future. Then tell me what I need to know to be an effective teacher for you—what do I need to do to meet your needs as a student?

Here are a couple example responses that Ms. Cone received from her students:

- *I would like you to know that I read books only when its concerning my grade and that I am a very slow reader. I would like you to know that I am shy to . . . read in front of people because I am afraid if they are going to laugh at me and hurts me deeply and makes my fear worse. (Nailah)*
- *I am not the greatest reader or writer in the world. I tend to studder alot when I read out loud and I sound slow. But when I read to myself I read ok. I have never really complited a hole book. I allway stop. I just hope to read and complete a interesting book in this class. The only one book I have read completely from front to back is Romeo and Juliet. I love to read Shakespers. (Maritza)*

Regardless of whether you decide to use a papier-mâché dinosaur or a writing prompt, the key takeaway is the importance of using the first day of your class to invite students to share their experiences and to communicate to students that you care about them and their unique perspectives.

Regardless of our best intentions, there are challenges and potential pitfalls involved. Setting a "supportive tone" is not a one-and-done effort; it requires continual effort. Indeed, if a student who shared on day one his intense fear of reading aloud only to find on day two that we failed to remember this and moved forward with a favorite read-aloud activity, then we have sent the exact opposite message of what was intended:

> I'll invite your perspective but won't really hear what you say. I'll ask you to trust me to take risks and then . . . betray that trust.

Some of the pitfalls are not as overt as this example. Indeed, many of the hazards are much subtler. Consequently, it is helpful to become actively aware of potential hazards, so you can proactively address them and thereby maximize the potential benefits to your students' confidence and willingness to take the risks necessary to think and act creatively.

## Anticipating and Addressing Potential Hazards

One of the biggest hazards involved in establishing a classroom environment conducive to supporting student creativity is the unintended creativity-stifling messages we sometimes send to our students. This particular hazard is challenging because sometimes what we believe is beneficial is experienced by some students in the opposite way we intended.

Consider the use of classroom data walls. Data walls are used in elementary, middle, and high school classrooms to visually display and monitor student progress on key performance outcomes (e.g., reading, math). Some teachers develop their data walls around themes to make them more inviting and interesting for students.

The potential themes teachers use for data walls are highly varied and limited only by one's imagination. Example themes include rising not-air balloons, rocket ships lifting off, running shoes in a race, animals climbing a tree, passengers on a cruise ship, movement on a sports field, and so on.

Students are given some kind of marker that signifies their individual progress (e.g., running shoe that they design, or some other icon related to the overall theme of the data wall). By personalizing the markers of performance on the data wall,[4] teachers hope to engage students and help motivate continued improvement.

In addition to using data walls to try to motivate student progress; teachers, administrators, and anyone who visits the classroom can use the data wall to get a quick snapshot of whole class performance and growth. Students can also use the data walls to monitor progress on everything from performance on academic quizzes and tests to attendance and classroom behavior.

Given these potential benefits of the data wall, why might it pose a hazard to supporting creative expression? First, it is important to stress that the use of data walls will not necessarily stifle student creativity. Rather, it is more about how students experience the data walls and what those data walls may (inadvertently) communicate to students that will determine whether a particular data wall will negatively impact a student's creative expression.

### An Example

Let's take a closer look at a data wall in action. Doing so will help to identify the potential pitfalls and consider options for addressing them. Imagine a middle school language arts teacher who has decided to use a data wall to motivate student engagement and monitor progress on his students' demonstrated understanding of literary terms.

After teaching a particular literary term, the teacher has students complete a five-minute "quick check"—assessing whether the students can accurately use the literary concept by coming up with their own creative use of it (e.g., come up with your own example of onomatopoeia; provide a novel example of foreshadowing).

The teacher designed a thematic data wall that represents a giant book of literary terms. Each student designed a small bookmark that included his or her initials and favorite literary character. All students start on the bottom of the book-themed data wall (labeled "preface") and move up the book wall, chapter by chapter, each time they accurately complete the five-minute quick check. The wall is divided into five sections, with five chapters in each section.

The teacher made the process even more enticing by letting students know that each time they accurately complete a check-in in the allotted time they will earn five minutes of "choice time" that they can use to read, play a game on their tablets, or quietly work on some other choice activity. And the first student to reach a new section receives an inexpensive item of their choice, paid for by the teacher, from the monthly book order or school store.

Students likely will be very excited by this idea. Even students who typically do not enjoy reading may have their interest sparked by the possibility of earning choice time and potentially obtaining something from the book order form or school store. When the teacher unveils the data wall he notes,

> I want you to think of this like a game and have fun learning about literature! I also want you to be creative and come up with your own accurate examples of these literary terms! By monitoring your own progress, this is one way you can take charge of your own learning and make it meaningful!

Although the teacher's goals include cultivating students' engagement, creativity, and self-monitoring of progress, the way the teacher is using this data wall can actually undermine engagement and student creativity.

The biggest hazards this data wall poses are the messages it sends. Although the teacher told his students that he wants them to treat the data wall like a game, the way the wall works in practice sends the following messages:

- *Mistakes should be avoided;*
- *Completing the assignment quickly is more important than taking the time you need to explore different uses of literary terms;*
- *Avoid incorrect responses if you want to get rewarded with free time and prizes from the school score; and*

- *Your progress (or lack thereof) will be publicly displayed for judgment and comparison.*

Taken together these messages can work against students' willingness to take the risks necessary for creative expression (Amabile, 1996; Beghetto, 2013; Hennessey, 2017). Indeed, as Hennessey (2017), has explained:

> the expectation that one's work will be judged and compared . . . may well be the most deleterious extrinsic constraint of all . . . because . . . competition often combines aspects of other "killers" of motivation and creativity, including expected reward and expected evaluation. (p. 348)

If students believe it is too hazardous to risk trying something new because it may take too much time or turn out to be incorrect, then it is understandable if they choose the safer path of a more conventional response. Consequently, creative expression suffers.

In addition to undermining students' willingness for creative expression, there are various other potential negative consequences of such an activity. Because student progress is displayed in a highly visible way, some students may develop an avoidant orientation toward this task, fearing that they may appear incompetent or less able than their peers.

Students who develop an avoidant orientation will do a range of things to avoid appearing incompetent (Midgely, 2002), including:

- cheating,
- trying to come up with excuses in advance of the task to account for lower levels of performance (e.g., "This is stupid, I'm not wasting my time on it!"), and
- engaging in disruptive or other negative behaviors to avoid the task.

These highly visible social comparisons therefore can negatively impact all students, even high-performing students. A high school English teacher, Agustin Morales, explained how a data wall negatively impacted one of his top students who did poorly on a test, which resulted in her being placed at the bottom of his data wall (Jaffe, 2014). He reports how later, in a writing assignment, the student wrote "how sad she was, how depressed she was because she'd scored negatively on it. She felt stupid" (Jaffe, 2014).

Data walls make the stakes very high—perhaps too high—when it comes to creative expression. Students who take the risk of creative expression and find themselves shamed by the experience, may end up abandoning their creative aspirations (Beghetto & Dilley, 2016).

It's true that students need honest and sometimes difficult-to-hear feedback if they are ever to develop the competence necessary for creative expression (see chapter 7). They also need lower-stakes situations, which encourage them to practice, fail, receive instructional support, and try again.

Developing the resilience to face the harsh realities of a cruel world does not come from exposing students to cruelty. Rather, given that students are still developing their creative confidence (Bandura, 1997; Beghetto, 2013), it is important to provide them with opportunities to:

- *take reasonable risks,*
- *receive honest and supportive feedback, and*
- *have a chance to develop the confidence necessary for withstanding set-backs and failures.*

## Maximizing Benefits

Having explored some potential hazards, it may be helpful to quickly highlight some of the key takeaways from this chapter to help ensure that you are maximizing the potential benefits of establishing a creativity-supportive learning environment:

***Recognize that potential alone is not enough.*** Just because your students have the potential to think and act creatively doesn't mean they will be willing to do so. Creative expression is a risk. Students therefore need to feel capable of taking such risks, recognize the value in doing so, and feel supported when they make mistakes and experience setbacks and struggles.

***Help students to develop their creative confidence.*** Creative confidence, like other forms of confidence beliefs (Bandura, 1997), develops from encouragement from teachers, from watching peers (who they can relate to) engage in creative expression, and from successful experiences with creative learning activities.

***Provide opportunities to recognize the value of creative expression.*** We can help students recognize the personal and social value of creative expression by having them actively reflect on and discuss how their own creative expression contributes to themselves and others.

***Monitor the kinds of messages being sent by classroom activities.*** Creativity supportive learning experiences send the following messages to students (see also Bandura, 1997; Beghetto, 2013, 2018; Dweck, 2006; Midgley, 2002):

- *The main goal of this activity is for everyone to develop and share different ideas, perspectives, and insights;*
- *The process sometimes gets messy, frustrating, and confusing, and that's okay;*

- *Asking for help is a sign of strength, effort is a sign of learning;*
- *Expect to struggle, and test your limits, and know it's okay to have fun;*
- *You can work alone, or with each other, join groups or leave them;*
- *It's okay to make mistakes, to start over, and to try something completely new;*
- *Follow your interests, take risks, challenge yourselves;*
- *Play to your strengths and explore your weaknesses; and*
- *We will make mistakes, but we will learn from those mistakes.*

***Frequently check in with your students.*** As with all human behavior, there's usually a gap between what is intended and what is actually experienced (Argyris & Schön, 1974). Even our most well-intended efforts can be experienced in surprising ways by students. It is therefore important that we frequently check in with students and provide multiple ways for them to share their comments, concerns, and questions with us about any aspect of their learning experience (see also chapter 7).

## SUMMARIZING ACTION PRINCIPLE

***If*** **you want to support students in moving from creative potential to creative behavior,** ***then*** **we need to design classroom learning environments that encourage rather than inadvertently suppress creative expression.**
There are several things we can do to help ensure that our students experience our classrooms as supportive of their creative expression. This includes helping students develop their confidence beliefs and make connections between their creative efforts and the outcomes of those efforts.

In addition to providing opportunities for students to develop their creative confidence and recognize the value of creative expression, we also need to monitor how students are *actually* experiencing our classroom environment. This requires shifting our perspective to our students' experience.

Indeed, no matter how well intended our efforts, we never fully know how students are experiencing in our classroom unless we take the time to check. This can be done by having students share their perspectives with "exit slips," anonymous drop boxes, or any way for students to quickly and frequently share their perspectives and experience.

Developing a creative classroom is not magic, but it does take persistence and effort. Fortunately, this effort is not difficult. Rather, it takes a shared commitment between students and teachers to frequently, honestly, and openly reflect on and discuss how the expectations for taking creative risks are being experienced by everyone and what can be done to provide needed supports.

## NOTES

1. The description of this student is based on an actual student who a preservice teacher, in one of my university courses, observed and worked with as part of a clinical field placement.

2. These rating scales and follow-up items are based on recommendations and similar examples provided in Bandura (2006); Beghetto (2018); Beghetto & Karwowski (2017).

3. Example retrieved from http://gallery.carnegiefoundation.org/collections/castl_ k12/jcone/index.html.

4. Most teachers are aware of and adhere to FERPA (Family Educational Rights and Privacy Act) requirements to protect identifying and academic information of students when using data walls. This is why teachers typically avoid using full names and, instead, use initials, first names only, assigned numbers, or student-decorated indicators. Still, there can be tricky issues involved when protecting students' privacy. It is therefore always best to check such practices. https://www.washingtonpost.com/ news/answer-sheet/wp/2014/02/21/how-some-school-data-walls-violate-u-s-privacy-law/?utm_term=.959f17a0e253

*Chapter Seven*

# The Beautiful Risk of Assessing for Creativity

I'd rather learn from one bird how to sing than teach 10,000 stars how not to dance.

—E. E. Cummings

A truism in education is: That which matters gets assessed. Where does this leave creativity? Can you assess creativity? And if you can, should you? The purpose of this chapter is to address these questions. As will be discussed, designing assessments with creativity in mind is an important aspect of supporting creativity in the classroom.

Assessing creativity, however, is a risk. There are several hazards involved that need to be monitored and minimized in order to ensure that your assessment practices are actually supporting creativity rather than suppressing it. Assessing creativity in a way that complements your instructional practices and benefits students' creative learning requires changing the way we sometimes think about classroom assessment.

## ASSESSING CREATIVITY IN THE CLASSROOM

When it comes to assessing creativity in the classroom the first thing to keep in mind is the importance of distinguishing between assessment *of* creativity versus assessment *for* creativity.[1] Figure 7.1 highlights the differences between these two approaches.

| TYPE | Description | Typical Uses | Example |
|------|-------------|--------------|---------|
| <br><br>*Assessment*<br>*of*<br>*Creativity* | Determine the amount or level of creativity expressed (usually in comparison to others) | Identify different levels of creative expression or accomplishment between people;<br><br>Compare creative expression amongst people;<br><br>Used by researchers to make determinations of more or less creative expression between people. | A panel of experts judges the creativity of poems written by a group of people—ranking the creativity of each poem in relation to the other poems (Amabile, 1996).<br><br>A group of people complete a creative activity and accomplishment checklist that indicates how frequently they engage in particular creative behaviors and the different levels of recognition for their accomplishments (Diedrich et al., 2017). |
| <br><br>*Assessment*<br>*for*<br>*Creativity* | Provide feedback on and recognition for engaging in creative behavior<br><br>Develop students' creative competence and confidence<br><br>Enable students to self-monitor their own creative expression | Encourage creative expression;<br><br>Increase awareness of creative behaviors;<br><br>Support confidence and self-regulation of creative behaviors; and<br><br>Promote higher levels of creative expression. | A teacher designs an assignment that provides credit for providing the correct answer to a word problem *and* at least two different ways of completing the problem.<br><br>A teacher uses exit slips that require students to monitor and reflect on their own creative confidence and performance (see also chapter 6).<br><br>A teacher uses a checklist to provide feedback on students developing creative expression (Beghetto, 2013). |

Figure 7.1.   Different Types of Creative Assessment

## Assessment *of* Creativity

As highlighted in figure 7.1 assessments of creativity tend to be focused on measuring different levels of creative performance, typically with respect to how people compare to each other. This focus is reflected in the measuring scales icon in figure 7.1.

Creativity researchers have developed and used a wide array of assessments to measure different levels of creative performance, including everything from creativity activity and achievement checklists (Diedrich et al., 2017) to expert ratings of creative products (Amabile, 1996).

Such measures typically are little use to teachers because they have been designed to differentiate different levels of creative performance for research purposes. In most cases, teachers do not need to assemble a panel of judges to assess the creativity represented in their students' creative products.[2] You'll therefore be focused on assessing *for* creativity.

## Assessment *for* Creativity

Unlike assessment *of* creativity, the goal of assessment *for* creativity is to encourage students' creative awareness and develop their creative competence. In this way, assessment for creativity involves providing feedback and recognition to students whenever they attempt to develop and share creative ideas, products, and actions.

As described in figure 7.1, assessment for creativity involves establishing expectations and credit for trying something new. The goal, like all growth-focused assessments, is to support the development of competence through continual improvement (Dweck, 2006; Midgley, 2002).

So how might this look in practice. Let's consider a few examples. Imagine a teacher who has provided students with five math practice problems for homework. The teacher adds the following instructions to the assignment,

> Each problem is worth a total of two points—you'll get one point for accurately solving each problem and you get another point if you come up with at least two ways of solving it.

In this way, students are provided credit not only for solving problems correctly, but also for trying to come up with creative solutions to each problem. This approach can be applied to most any subject. In language arts, for instance, students might get credit for summarizing the plot of a short story and additional credit for coming up with their own, unique plot twist.

In history, students might get credit for describing the causal factors of a historical event and additional credit for describing a historically plausible alternative. Whenever you provide credit for students who attempt to generate new and different ideas then you are formally communicating to them that you expect and value creative risk-taking in your classroom.

You can also use checklists to provide more direct feedback on students' efforts to generate creative ideas. Table 7.1 provides an example checklist that you and your students can use to identify different levels of creative expression.

As has been discussed elsewhere (Beghetto, 2013; Beghetto et al., 2015), the various levels of performance on creativity checklists and rubrics (like the one illustrated in table 7.1), can serve as a guide for you and your students to set goals prior to completing a task, to support creative expression during a task, and to reflect on and discuss creative performance following a task.

**Table 7.1.  Checklist of Creative Proficiency**

| Level | Teacher | Student |
|---|---|---|
| *Aspirational* (pro-c) | Student makes a significant creative contribution, something that would be expected from or recognized as creative by an accomplished professional or expert. | "I came up with something that is very creative and can make an important contribution to others. It is something that experts or professionals would recognize as creative." |
| Accomplished (surprising little-c) | The student uses a surprising, original, or substantially different way of meeting the criteria. | "I did something in a completely different way and it worked (or fit the expectations)." |
| Developing (little-c) | The student uses a slightly different way to meet the requirements of the assignment, activity, or task. | "I shared an idea or did something that was kind of new and it worked." |
| Emerging (mini-c) | The student tries doing something that is new and meaningful for them but not new to others; or tries a different approach, but doesn't meet requirements of the assignment, activity, or task. | "I tried doing something that is new for me, but not others. I tried something new, but it didn't work or didn't fit the expectations." |
| *No Attempt* (no-c) | Made no attempt to try something new or different. | "I didn't try to do something new." |

The top (Pro-c) and bottom (no-c) levels likely will be used infrequently as they represent opposite extremes (i.e., not trying to do anything creative vs. performing at a level beyond what is typically expected). Keeping these extremes on the checklist, however, can help in setting challenges for students.

The "no attempt" level, for instance, can be useful in setting more challenging goals for students who might be reluctant to take creative risks or who feel overwhelmed by the idea of "doing something creative." If you have students who are reluctant to take creative risks, you might encourage them by reminding them that they need not start out by trying to do something wildly creative.

I noticed that you didn't try doing something new on this assignment. Let's set a goal that you try something slightly new. Try something that is new for you, even if it isn't new for anyone else.

This kind of encouragement can help a student who is overwhelmed by the thought of "being creative" recognize that there is still value in doing something that is new and personally meaningful to them. Recall from chapter 2 that this form of mini-c personal creativity is not only a legitimate creative experience, but also a core aspect of learning creatively.

The aspirational levels of proficiency can help students think about what expert or highly accomplished creative performance might look like (Pro-c creativity). You can provide examples of what this might look like and encourage students to set aspirational goals of doing something that will make a positive and lasting contribution to others (recall the legacy challenges from chapter 5).

Prior to using this checklist, it is important to have a discussion with your students of what these different levels of creative expression might look like for a particular assignment, project, or task. The more examples and specifics about the examples, the better. The best examples would be samples of what students have done before.

Of course, if this is the first time you are using a checklist like this, then you'll need to discuss possibilities of what the final product might look like. Once students have developed an idea of different levels of creative performance, you can then have them use the checklist to set a goal for themselves prior to performing a particular task.

Then you can have them refer to this checklist as they start working on the task—encouraging them to make necessary adjustments (e.g., "This is a bit more difficult than I thought, but I'll still try to do something that is at least kind of new"). Finally, after completing the task, you can have them check the level of creative performance they feel they demonstrated in their work.

You can independently assess the work using the same checklist and then compare and discuss the ratings, including differences between your and their rating and how your students might continue to improve and challenge themselves (Beghetto, 2013).

Taken together, these examples provide a small sample of the possible ways that you might assess for creativity in your classroom. The key is to provide students with continual encouragement and feedback on their efforts. This includes inviting students to self-assess their own creative performance in relation to your feedback.

Assessing for creativity has the goal of helping to develop students' creative confidence and their creative competence. Indeed, helping students develop their creative metacognitive knowledge (i.e., knowledge about their creative strengths and weaknesses) will enable them to set more realistic and challenging goals and self-regulate their efforts when working on creative tasks (Beghetto & Karwowski, 2017; Kaufman & Beghetto, 2013).

## HOW TO TAKE THE BEAUTIFUL RISK

Assessing for creativity can be boiled down to one word: *Feedback*. In order to support the development of students' creative confidence and competence, they need opportunities to not only share their ideas, but also receive feedback on those ideas.

There are several considerations to take into account when providing feedback aimed at supporting student creativity. Doing so will help in anticipating and proactively addressing potential hazards and maximizing potential benefits. As discussed in chapter 2, the movement from mini-c insights to creative accomplishments requires testing out and receiving feedback on ideas from relevant audiences.

In the context of the classroom, teachers play a critical role in providing opportunities for students to receive and take action on that feedback. When it comes to feedback supportive of creative expression, there are two key considerations:

1. How feedback is *provided*, and
2. How feedback is *received*.

The first consideration pertains to the way you provide feedback to your students, including what specifically you are communicating to your students. And the second consideration, as was discussed in chapter 6, pertains to how students experience your feedback.

Consequently, when providing feedback on students' creative expression, the goal is to strike the right balance between honest and supportive, what has elsewhere been described as the *Goldilocks Principle* (Beghetto & Kaufman, 2007).

Just like Goldilocks encountered different temperatures of porridge in her search for the one that was "just right" for her, feedback can also be experienced as being: *too hot, too cold,* and *just right*. Being aware of the differences between these types of feedback can help ensure that you are striking the "just right" balance with your students.

### Feedback That Is Too Hot

In order to improve, students need to receive honest feedback (Black & Wiliam, 1998), which can sometimes be difficult to hear. Honest feedback, however, need not be harsh. Indeed, students who take a creative risk only to be mocked and made to feel like improvement is not possible likely will avoid or give up on taking such risks in the future (Beghetto & Dilley, 2016).

If feedback is too harsh it can haunt students—even many years later. Let's consider a couple examples.[3] Peggy Orenstein is an accomplished journalist and author who has described how she vividly recalls feedback that might be considered "too hot" from her prior schooling experience. She explains how she was able to clearly and quickly recall several instances of harsh feedback from her childhood:

> I recalled my beloved kindergarten teacher putting my drawing of the solar system into what was obviously the "bad" pile; being repeatedly, negatively compared to my musically gifted brother; being mocked for wrong answers as one of the few girls in eighth-grade accelerated math. (Orenstein 2011, p. 4)

You likely can recall similar instances in your own life. Such moments can have a lasting negative effect, particularly for students who have a creative interest in some area (e.g., singing, writing, science, art, math) and are still in the early phases of developing their competence (Beghetto & Dilley, 2016).

Such moments can occur whenever teachers or peers respond in an effort to be funny or sarcastic to a student's creative risk taking. It is worth noting that although teachers sometimes use sarcasm in an effort to connect with their students, doing so runs the risk of your students experiencing it in a harsh or demoralizing way. This is not surprising given that sarcasm literally means to "tear flesh."

Here's an example. A vignette from *The Rhode Island Schoolmaster* (De-Munn & Snow, 1865, p. 88) vividly describes how sarcasm can be experienced as harsh feedback. One day, a student named Jane who "cherished the idea of becoming a singer" started to sing with her classmates. Her teacher commented, "Jane, what are you trying to sing? The tune sung by the old cow when she died? What a discord!"

Her classmates laughed. And Jane immediately stopped singing, "dropped her head upon the desk, and the bitter tears ran down her cheeks" (DeMunn & Snow, 1865, p. 88). Jane experienced her teacher's attempt to "poke fun" as painful, harsh feedback. "To her the fact that the teacher ridiculed her efforts was evidence that she could never learn" (DeMunn & Snow, 1865, p. 88).

Seeing how Jane reacted, the teacher was sorry for the remark but thought Jane would soon forget about it. Unfortunately, "the remembrance of those words would always remain with Jane, to keep her, in future, from the vain attempt to sing" (DeMunn & Snow, 1865, p. 88).

As these two examples illustrate, harsh feedback can have a lasting impact and result in what has been called "creative mortification" (Beghetto, 2013), whereby students give up on pursuing their creative interests. One reason this can happen is because the remembrance of that experience serves as a painful reminder that they are not good enough.

Not all students who experience harsh feedback will abandon their creative pursuits. It is possible that some people can be motivated by such experiences. The important difference between those who are motivated and those who give up on creative pursuits seems to come down to how they experience those moments. If students experience shame from harsh feedback and believe there is no chance to get better, then they are likely to abandon their creative aspirations (Beghetto, 2014).

Although it is possible that some people can find motivation from such experiences (e.g., motivation to prove people wrong), they still need to believe that they can get better (Dweck, 2006) *and* they will also need the instructional and social supports necessary to do so. Given the potential hazards of feedback that is too hot, it's important that we monitor how our students experience that feedback.

## Feedback That Is Too Cold

The flipside of overly harsh feedback is feedback that lacks the honest critique necessary for improvement (Beghetto & Kaufman, 2007). Such feedback is "too cold" because it lacks the warmth of reality. Although lavishing unwarranted praise on students may have the intent of trying to encourage and support students, there are hazards in doing so. Specifically, our well-intended efforts to praise students can backfire.

One way that praise can backfire is if students recognize that the praise they are receiving is unwarranted. Rather than having the intended impact of boosting confidence, excessively praising students for mediocre performance can, somewhat ironically, undermine students' beliefs in their competence (Bandura, 1997, p. 102).

A student may feel like, "Wow, I must *really* be terrible if my teacher feels the need to keep pretending like I'm good at this, when we both know that I'm not." Of course, not all students recognize that the excessive praise they receive is unwarranted. Some believe that it accurately reflects their ability, which can also be problematic (Kruger & Dunning, 1999).

Consequently, another way praise can backfire is when young people's confidence has been unrealistically boosted well beyond their *current* level of competence. Doing so can result in a double whammy of negative outcomes. Not only will young people eventually come up against the painful reality of their actual level of competence, but the well-intended supporters who unrealistically boosted their confidence will also be discredited. As Bandura (1997) has explained:

> To raise unrealistic beliefs of personal capabilities, however, only invites failures that will discredit the persuaders and further undermine the recipient's beliefs in their capabilities. (p. 101)

Televised "talent" shows are perhaps one of the most common and public examples of how unrealistically high levels of confidence can come quickly crashing down in the face of honest critique. The consequence of falling from the heights of unrealistically boosted levels of confidence, or of failing to be recognized for one's perceived talent, can be experienced as painfully as the sting from overly harsh feedback. As Kaufman (2016) has cautioned:

> At some point, reality will hit and it will feel like the emperor's new clothes; they will wonder why no one was ever honest with them. Or, conversely, they may end up wondering why the world never appreciates their talents. (p. 259)

It is therefore important to keep in mind that although we may feel that providing praise is a good thing, if our praise is not warranted, then we are doing a disservice to young people. This does not mean that we should withhold praise that is warranted. Indeed, failing to acknowledge successful performance can also undermine students' confidence (Bandura, 1997).

Consequently, when providing creativity-supportive feedback we should strive to strike that "just right" balance of providing an honest appraisal of students' current strengths and weaknesses.

## Just Right Feedback

Whenever students take the risk of sharing a unique idea, perspective, or behavior it is important that we ensure that the feedback they receive is experienced as honest and supportive (Bandura, 1998; Beghetto & Kaufman, 2007; Wiliam, 2011). Such feedback should, at a minimum, focus on communicating the following:

**Appreciation.** Thanking students for taking the risk of sharing unique ideas, insights, or actions (e.g., "Thank you for sharing that idea. Hearing different perspectives on this topic can really help us consider it from different angles").

**Specificity.** How students specifically have put a unique spin on the activity or assignment (e.g., "I really like how your metaphor provides a unique way of describing why we need common denominators when adding fractions, but don't need them when dividing fractions").

**Honesty.** The feedback you provide to students needs to be honest. Remember, honest doesn't mean cruel or harsh. Rather, honest means providing feedback that lets students know their *current* level of competence and highlights areas that can be worked on.

Prefacing your feedback with "What if . . ." can be a powerful way of providing an honest critique to students (Beghetto, 2018). "What if . . ." signifies one possibility and may be experienced as more helpful than a potentially more accusatory critique that start with "Why didn't you . . ." Consider the difference in these two example critiques:

- *"**What if** you more directly connected your unique explanation to the main theme of the story? I'm not seeing the connection. . ." [Can be experienced as more supportive]*
- *"**Why didn't you** more directly connect your unique explanation to the main theme of the story? I'm not seeing the connection . . ." [Can be experienced as more accusatory]*

**Improvement.** When assessing for creativity, your feedback should always include specific ideas for how students might continue to improve. Improvement-focused feedback highlights what next steps can be taken, regardless of whether:

- Students did an outstanding job with a task *(e.g., "Nice work! Now, how might you expand this project to include . . .")* or
- Struggled with the task *(e.g., "I know this was a very challenging assignment for you . . . if you were to do it again, what's at least one small thing you could do to put your own unique twist on it . . .").*

Taken together these features of feedback will help ensure that you are striking the "just right" balance between supporting students and providing an honest critique of their current strengths and weaknesses. In addition to monitoring how your feedback is both provided to and received by students, you also want to establish a classroom environment that encourages and models openness to feedback.

The best way to do this is to start with yourself. Indeed, a common theme stressed throughout this book is how can we expect our students to take beautiful risks if we are not willing to do so ourselves.

## Start with Yourself

Modeling for students how to provide and receive feedback is one of the best ways to establish a classroom environment supportive of creative expression. Indeed, assessing *for* creativity is not only about providing feedback to students, but also establishing opportunities for your students to provide feedback to you.

The benefits of providing creativity-supportive feedback to others not only helps the person receiving the feedback but also can benefit the person providing feedback. This is because people who know how to provide useful critiques tend to be more likely to be able to generate new and creative insights themselves (Gibson & Mumford, 2013).

The effects of creativity-supportive feedback can accrue and benefit everyone involved by establishing a climate of continual improvement and beautiful risk taking. So how might this look in your classroom? One way is to start by using the "My Teaching Best" protocol (adapted from Beghetto, 2016a; Roberts, Dutton, Spreitzer, Heaphy, & Quinn, 2005; Roberts, Spreitzer, Dutton, Quinn, Heaply, & Barker, 2005).

## My Teaching Best Protocol

This protocol is a simple, strength-based, and improvement-focused approach to obtaining evaluative feedback on your teaching. Not only will it help you identify key strengths and potential areas of improvement, it also teaches your students how to provide improvement-focused feedback to others.

The following questions can help you decide when and how you might use this protocol in your own classroom.

***When do I use it?*** It is a good idea to use this protocol early and often during the school year. Although it is ideal to start at the beginning of the year (e.g., "In this class we will be providing feedback to each other. And we will start with me."), it is also okay to start using this protocol at any point in the school year (e.g., "I've been providing feedback to you on your work. And you have been providing feedback to each other. Starting now, I'm going to have you also provide feedback to me.")

Regardless of when you start, the key is to provide students with multiple opportunities to provide feedback any time you are trying out a new lesson, when you are interested in improving an existing one, or even if you want to test your assumptions about one of your favorite lessons. In this way, you can receive feedback that is helpful for your own growth and creative expression.

***How do I use it?*** This protocol has two simple but powerful steps. The first step is to let students know, prior to teaching a new lesson or activity, that you will be inviting their feedback. You will further want to let them know whether you want feedback on your teaching or the activity itself.

Then, immediately after the lesson, both you and your students complete a strength-based statement and an improvement-focused statement, here are some example statements that you can tailor for your own specific purposes:

**Example strength-based starters:**

- [Student] *"You were at your teaching best when you . . . [explain what they thought you did best in your teaching during this lesson]"*
- [Teacher] *"I was at my teaching best when I . . . [explain what you think you did best during your teaching of this lesson]"*
- [Student/teacher] *"This activity was best when . . . [explain the best thing about this activity]"*
- [Student/teacher] *"The best part of this assignment was . . . [explain the best thing about this assignment]"*

**Example improvement-focused starters:**

- [Student/teacher] *"What if [you/I] tried . . . [explain an idea for how to improve]"*
- [Student/teacher] *"What if the activity was modified so that it . . . [explain how to make an improvement]"*
- [Student/teacher] *"What if the assignment was changed by . . . [explain how to make an improvement]"*

You only need to use one strength-based and one improvement-focused prompt and tailor it to what you are seeking feedback on (e.g., your teaching, an activity you designed, an assignment). If, for instance, you want feedback on what your students think you do best when teaching, you can use the "teaching best" starters. If, on the other hand, you want feedback on an activity or assignment, you can use those prompts.

The second step involves reflecting on these statements. After you and your students have a chance to respond to one strength-based and one improvement-focused statement, collect and review them. You can review the statements on your own or with your students. The aim is to identify common themes as well as differences.

Some of the most interesting and potentially transformative insights will be in how you and your students viewed aspects of your teaching or learning assignments differently. Based on your review of these comments, you can then decide how you might make changes moving forward. In this way, the feedback will serve as a highly tailored and embedded form of instructional feedback (Wiliam, 2011).

Most importantly, let your students know what you learned from their feedback and how it will impact your teaching moving forward. Although this is a simple exercise, it takes courage. It takes courage because you are allowing yourself to be vulnerable by inviting feedback on something you are still developing or trying to improve.

It also takes courage on the part of your students because you are asking them to provide honest feedback to you. Students typically are not invited to provide this kind of direct feedback to their teachers. There will be uncertainty both on your part and on the part of your students. In this way, inviting students to provide feedback on your teaching is a beautiful risk because both you and your students need to step into uncertainty.

By starting with yourself, you can model the importance of being open to receiving honest and supportive feedback. This helps to send the message that providing feedback is a responsibility of *everyone* in your classroom.

## SUMMARIZING ACTION PRINCIPLE

**If you want to encourage and recognize creative expression in your classroom, *then* you need to assess *for* creativity.**

As discussed, assessment for creativity is all about providing feedback that is focused on improvement because it blends honesty with supportive insights on how to improve. Although there are hazards involved whenever we give or receive helpful and supportive feedback, the benefits of doing so outweigh the costs.

By starting with ourselves, we can model to our students how being open to receiving improvement-focused feedback can help identify current strengths and actionable areas in need of improvement. Such feedback goes beyond empty platitudes (e.g., "Super job!" or "Still needs work") and toward providing information that communicates appreciation, specificity, honesty, and what steps can and will be taken to improve.

When your students see you inviting feedback and acting on it, then they may be more likely to welcome it themselves. Moreover, because you are involving them in the process, you can help demystify feedback. As a result, you can transform assessment *for* creativity from something that is mysterious or rarely seen into a routine practice of your classroom.

## NOTES

1. This distinction is similar to the way classroom assessment experts (see Stiggins, 2002) have differentiated between assessments *of* and *for* learning. See also Sefton-Green's (2011) discussion of evaluating creative learning for a broader perspective on this topic.

2. As mentioned in chapter 2, this expert panel methodology, formally called the Consensual Assessment Technique (Amabile, 1996), is typically used by researchers and involves experts independently ranking the creativity represented by a set of

products created by a group of people. Inter-rater reliabilities are calculated and used to check the consistency of the ratings, and the validity comes from the expertise of the panel. Although teachers would rarely need to use this time-intensive and formal type of assessment, there may be some occasions where a modified version of this could be used (e.g., judging for a contest or competition).

3. The two examples and discussion of those examples in this section are adapted from Beghetto (2013) and Beghetto & Dilley (2016).

*Chapter Eight*

# The Beautiful Risk
# of Using Creative Curricula

Have no fear of perfection, you'll never reach it.

—Salvador Dali

Perhaps your school has invested in a makerspace or you are being encouraged to incorporate design thinking into your teaching. Regardless of the curricular technique, tool, or trend, it seems like each year some new curricular experience emerges that promises creative learning experiences, such as:

- *The maker movement* (i.e., providing opportunities for students to create using physical materials in a designated "makerspace" in or outside your classroom);
- *gamification* (infusing principles of gaming into educational experiences);
- *design thinking* (using principles of the design process to create something or solve a problem);
- *coding & robotics* (teaching students programming skills and how to design and use robots);
- *virtual and augmented reality* (technologies that provide experiences creating and interacting with virtual and augmented worlds); and
- *STEAM initiatives* (integrating the arts into science, technology, engineering, and mathematics).

These and related efforts are often aimed at promoting student and teacher engagement, creative learning, and innovation. The list of such options continues to grow and change with each passing year.

Trying to get up to speed and keep up with each new technology, technique, or instructional strategy can quickly become overwhelming. It is therefore important to try to identify what is common across these options. If you can get a handle on the underlying framework or structure, then it is easier to recognize how each of these seemingly new and different options can be thought of as a form of *creative curriculum.*

Creative curricula refer to curricular technologies, techniques, or experiences that have the *potential* to provide students with opportunities to meet preestablished criteria by sharing their own unique perspectives, developing their own approach to doing something, or coming up with their own creative outcomes.

Transforming the potential of creative curricula into actual creative outcomes starts with taking the beautiful risk of incorporating new tools, techniques, and experiences into your classroom. But simply incorporating a new approach is not enough. As discussed in chapter 2, creativity researchers have long recognized that no technique, strategy, or technology will result in creativity (Barron, 1969).

Rather, as with all creative endeavors, using creative curricula effectively requires establishing the conditions necessary to increase the chances that they will encourage creative experiences and outcomes. The purpose of this chapter is to help clarify the underlying structure of creative curricular experiences and offer insights into how you might take the beautiful risk of using creative curricula in your classroom.

## UNDERSTANDING CREATIVE CURRICULA

The word curriculum has Latin origins in the word *currere,* which means "to run." And the curriculum serves as the *course* on which the race is run. This is an apt metaphor as teaching the academic curriculum can, indeed, feel like you're always in a race to get to the end of one topic so you can start another. But these early origins also speak to the game-like and challenging features of an experience.

Taking the beautiful risk of using creative curricula can be thought of as providing experiences that immerse students in an enjoyable and challenging learning activity. The benefit of taking this view of the curriculum is that it can serve as a powerful lens for seeing new opportunities in how you might design creative teaching and learning activities for your students.

Creative curricula combine opportunities for original expression within the structure and constraints of specific guidelines and learning criteria. In this way, creative curricula map on to standard definitions of creativity (chapter

2) and also provide openings for creative expression in the context of predetermined criteria (chapter 4).

Figure 8.1 provides a visual metaphor of this blend (adapted from Beghetto, 2017a). As illustrated in figure 8.1, creative curricula represent a blend between *predetermined* and *to-be-determined* elements. The predetermined elements represent the guidelines, criteria, and any other features that are defined by you and the particular type of curricular activity. When using a makerspace, for instance, you will have students work within an established set of guidelines and criteria.

The to-be-determined elements represent what students will contribute to or create in the experience. When students learn how to code, for instance, they need to work within the constraints of the particular platform or coding language, but they will still have opportunities to develop their own designs.

## How > What

The how is greater than the what when it comes to creative curricula. Indeed, no matter how promising a new curricular tool or technique, there are no guarantees it will result in creative outcomes. The potential of any curriculum can only be realized in how it is used.

The flashiest makerspace on the planet can quickly turn into nothing more than a glorified, high-tech setting for rote instruction. Whereas a simple stick of chalk, when put to good use, can unleash powerful creative insights. It all comes down to how curricular tools, technologies, and techniques are used.

Simply stated, when it comes to creative curricular experiences, *how* you use curricular tools, techniques, and experiences is more important than the specific features, equipment, or techniques you use. As with any beautiful risk, there are various potential hazards involved in using creative curricula.

The following section provides key considerations for how you might navigate these hazards to ensure that you use curricular tools, technologies, and experiences in a way that supports your students' (and your own) creative expression.

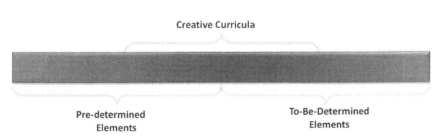

Figure 8.1.   Blended Elements of Creative Curricula

## HOW TO TAKE THE BEAUTIFUL RISK

Incorporating a new technology, technique, or learning experience in your curriculum is always a bit risky. Not only do you need to invest time in getting up to speed with what you are doing, there is always some level of uncertainty about whether trying something new will work out and be worth your and your students' time. Of course, there is also risk involved in not changing the way you currently teach.

If you want to provide opportunities for you and your students to develop your students' ability to respond creatively to uncertainty, then you need to be willing to take the beautiful risk of *leaning into* the uncertainty of trying something new (Beghetto, 2016a). This is not about leaping off the curricular cliff edge, rather it's about taking small, well thought-out risks in an effort to provide creative learning opportunities.

Regardless of the type of creative curricula you design or use, there are a few potential hazards to navigate to increase the chances of creative learning experiences and outcomes.

### Navigating Potential Hazards

As mentioned in the opening of this chapter, the rapid proliferation of new options for teaching and learning can leave you feeling behind the curve. New gadgets, techniques, and learning experiences often emerge on the educational scene before anyone has a clear sense of how or why they might be incorporated into the classroom.

Consequently, a key hazard to navigate is to ensure that creative curricula experiences do not simply become a means to their own end, but rather serve as a means for students to put tools, technologies, and learning spaces to creative ends.

Having students using computer-aided design software to more precisely calculate and model the perimeter of an actual school garden they are designing would be an example of using a tool as a means for accomplishing a more creative end. This differs from the typical approach to teaching academic skills and concepts, which tend to represent a means to their own end (Beghetto et al., 2015).

This is not to say that there is no value in teaching skills or content as a means to their own end. If this is your goal, that's fine. But, if you want to teach in a way that enables students to creatively use what they have learned, then students need opportunities to apply those skills and concepts to creative ends. Failing to navigate this hazard can result in several related hazards, including:

**Missed opportunities for creative expression.** New technologies and potentially creative curricular experiences can, somewhat ironically, turn out to be missed opportunities for creative expression. If the goal of spending time on a new technology is simply to learn about the tool and not how to use the tool creatively, then it represents a missed opportunity.

Indeed, scripted and superficial experiences (e.g., just play around with it; make something, it doesn't matter what it is) become problematic if students never have an opportunity to put their skills and knowledge to meaningful use.

Recall from chapter 2 that aimless exploration and unconstrained originality are not creativity. Creativity requires opportunities for original expression in a meaningful context, which includes task constraints and criteria for success.

**A disconnect between creative curricular experiences and your existing curricular responsibilities.** Similar to the missed opportunity for creative expression, when new technologies and instructional techniques become a means to their own end, then the chances of meaningfully connecting them to your existing academic curriculum become undermined.

Consequently, such efforts end up competing with rather than complementing your primary curricular responsibilities. When this happens, it becomes increasingly difficult to justify spending time on such activities and experiences.

**The macaroni art phenomenon.** Finally, when creative curricula are used as a means to their own end, then there will be little to show for the time and effort that you and your students devoted to the experience.

An example would be to have students make some random design on a 3-D printer, just so they can learn how to print using the 3-D printer. Such an experience is little more than a high-tech version of "macaroni art." Although the experience can be fun and provide students with an opportunity to make a design using a new technology, there is little lasting value.

One way to address this problem is follow up the high-tech macaroni art project with a more meaningful and creative use of the technology (e.g., using the 3-D printer to make key chains for a student-led fundraiser). In this way, the students can learn the technology *and* learn to put it to creative use.

In sum, there is nothing wrong with spending time on an enjoyable curricular experience or teaching students features of new technologies. If, however, you and your students are going to devote precious curricular time to it, then it makes sense to maximize the potential benefits of taking the beautiful risk of using creative curricula.

## Maximizing Benefits

Creative curricular experiences are designed to provide students with an opportunity to develop and express their creative insights and take creative action in the context of a supportive structure. When designing or using creative curricula in your classroom, there are a few considerations to keep in mind that can help ensure that they complement rather than compete with your existing curricular responsibilities.

The following checklist provides a way for you to quickly determine whether a particular creative curricular experience can simultaneously support student learning and provide students with opportunities to develop their creative competence. Table 8.1 provides an example checklist that you can use to help you make decisions about how you might use or modify a particular creative curricular experience with your students.

The creative curricular elements listed in table 8.1 represent a starter list of key elements. You can (and should) modify this list—removing or adding elements that fit with your specific situation and curricular goals. At this point, it may be helpful to see an example of how this checklist might be put into action.

### An Example

Escape rooms are a popular form of entertainment, which involve a group of people working together to solve a set of puzzles, within a specified amount of time. The puzzles represent a larger theme or narrative (e.g., solve this mystery, escape from an island with an active volcano, prevent a zombie apocalypse).

Educators have started adapting escape rooms to be used in their classroom (Wiemker, Elumir, & Clare, 2015). Designing and using escape rooms in your classroom *can* represent a creative curricular experience, but like all creative curricula there are hazards involved.

Incorporating an escape room in your curriculum without taking the extra step of ensuring that it includes elements like those listed in table 8.1 can result in an experience that lacks a meaningful connection to your academic curriculum, represents a missed opportunity for creative expression, and leaves you and your students with little to show for the time and effort you invested.

Alternatively, if you use the checklist in table 8.1, you can increase the chances that you design an engaging and meaningful creative learning experience for your students. Let's move through the checklist as a way to demonstrate how you can use and modify features of escape rooms to better meet the creative curricular elements listed in the checklist.

**Table 8.1.** Creative Curricula Checklist

| PRESENT | | ELEMENT | MODIFICATIONS |
|---|---|---|---|
| Yes | No | Key elements of creative curricular experiences | If not present, what kinds of modifications might you make to ensure that this element is included? |

**Provides creative openings.** Students have opportunities to identify their own problems, develop their own ways of doing things, create their own solutions, or produce their own unique outcomes.

**Connects to academic content.** Students are required to use or demonstrate key academic content or skills when participating in this curricular experience.

**Clear criteria for success.** The experience has clear criteria for success, including; what specifically students are required to demonstrate, how much time they have, how they can obtain help if they need it, and any other expectations or guidelines for participating in this curricular experience.

**Multiple opportunities for student feedback.** Students have opportunities to receive and provide feedback multiple times throughout the process. Students also have opportunities to receive feedback from multiple sources (peers, their teachers, and relevant audiences outside of their classroom).

**Opportunities for multiple iterations.** Students have multiple opportunities to try out their ideas, products, actions; receive feedback; reflect on that feedback; make necessary changes; and repeat the process.

**Work can be exhibited.** Student work is publicly exhibited and maintained so that it can contribute to and inspire the work of others.

**Focus on process.** Although the experience may result in creating a tangible product, the focus is on the creative learning process. Students have an opportunity to reflect on and discuss what they have learned from the process, what they learned about creativity, and what they learned about themselves—especially if they ran into setbacks, they made mistakes, or their products/projects didn't work.

**Informs instruction.** There are multiple opportunities to gather information that can help guide your instructional decisions and help you make timely adjustments to support students.

**Provides creative openings.** Escape rooms offer a mini-c creative experience, because participants often experience new and personally meaningful
insights. Beyond a mini-c experience, the typical escape room provides
limited opportunities for creative expression. Indeed, there are preset puzzles, with predetermined solutions, and typically a predetermined method
for arriving at those solutions.

Consequently, the "creative openings" element is not fully met and
requires some modification. There are several ways that a typical escape
room can be modified to transform it into a creative escape challenge. One
way is to include puzzles that have multiple solutions.

Students, for instance, might be required to solve a math problem using at least three different ways in order to move on to the next portion of
the escape challenge. An even better way to meet this element is to invite
students to design the puzzles themselves. You can start by introducing
students to escape rooms and walk them through a few sample puzzles (see
Wiemker, Elumir, & Clare, 2015, for an overview).

Next you can discuss the design components of the experience (e.g.,
backstory, puzzles, time limit, rules) and then have them design their own
(smaller scale) escape challenges for peers, other students in the school, or
even the broader community.

This type of modification would ensure that the escape room experience
provides students with creative opportunities to design their own creative
escape challenges, by coming up with their own theme, designing their
own puzzles and solutions, developing how the escape challenge will un-
fold, and inviting others to participate in the creative experience that they
have designed.

**Connects to academic content.** The most typical escape room experiences
do not connect to the academic curriculum. Educators, however, have
started designing and using escape rooms that involve academic content.
This involves adding learning goals and academic subject matter to the
puzzles they design and use in classroom-based escape rooms.

In this way, creative escape challenges can infuse a blend of various
subject areas (e.g., math, social studies, language arts, science) or focus
on a specific academic topic (e.g., the scarlet letter). By ensuring that the
puzzles focus on academic knowledge or skills, creative escape challenges
can provide students with opportunities to make connections to the academic content.

**Clear criteria for success.** As with any creative learning activity, establishing and making sure students understand the criteria for success is essential. If you are having students design their own creative escape experience,

you can develop a checklist of criteria that they would need to meet in their design, such as:

- *The specific academic content (e.g., mathematical order of operations) or skills (e.g., working collaboratively) that need to be included in the puzzles,*
- *The time limit for the entire challenge,*
- *The size of teams working on the puzzles, and*
- *Any other criteria or constraints you want to include.*

You might, for instance, have students working in teams of four or five. You can have each team design an escape challenge for the other teams. They would start by coming up with a backstory and theme (e.g., zombie apocalypse) and then design three puzzles (with your guidance) and establish a time limit for the entire experience (e.g., 15 minutes).

Alternatively, you could have the entire group design a larger escape challenge and have your students working in teams to design the components (i.e., backstory, puzzles). You can then use your classroom as an escape room and invite other classes or outside audiences (e.g., family members) to participate in what students have designed.

Regardless of the specifics, creative learning experiences require establishing and clearly communicating criteria for success, including: what specifically students are required to demonstrate, how much time they have, how they can obtain help if they need it, and any other expectations or guidelines for participating in this curricular experience.

**Multiple opportunities for student feedback.** Escape rooms, in themselves, provide limited opportunities for feedback other than the direct feedback of whether a person correctly solves a puzzle or not. Having your students design a creative escape room, on the other hand, can provide multiple opportunities to provide and receive feedback.

When, for instance, students are designing the escape challenge themes and puzzles you can make sure that they have opportunities to share their developing ideas with you, their peers, and others. As you may recall from chapter 2, the most direct way to help support the development of mini-c ideas into larger-c creative contributions is to have students share and receive feedback on their ideas.

Importantly, as discussed in chapter 7, students will also benefit from providing feedback to each other. In addition to providing feedback to students during the design phase of a creative escape challenge, you can also provide feedback to students during their participation in an escape challenge.

The K12 Lab of Stanford University's Design School, for instance, has developed a "puzzle room observational matrix"[1] that educators can use to assess students' demonstration of various skills while participating in a puzzle room. Some of these skills include:

- *giving and receiving help;*
- *demonstrating prosocial behaviors such as providing compliments;*
- *helping groups stay focused; and*
- *communication skills such as clear explanations and active listening.*

Educators can use, modify, or develop their own rubrics to provide improvement-focused feedback on how well students demonstrated key skills during the experience.

Finally, you can provide feedback to students after they have unveiled their creative escape challenge. One simple way of doing so is to have them hear strengths and *what if* suggestions for improvement.

**Opportunities for multiple iterations.** Feedback is essential, but it can quickly lose its power if students don't have an opportunity to learn from it and make necessary modifications. In the context of a creative escape room, for instance, you can provide multiple opportunities for students to test out their ideas; receive feedback; reflect on that feedback; make necessary changes; and repeat.

In addition to helping strengthen their design, multiple iterations help students recognize their creative strengths and address potential weaknesses. When designing creative escape challenges, students will need to have time to develop puzzles, test them out, and make revisions. Developing this kind of iterative mindset will put students in a better position to continually learn from their creative work.

Students may come to realize that creative work is never really finished (Corazza, 2016), but lives on and can continually be improved and modified. The same can be said for the creative curricula that you design and use in your own classroom. In this way, creative teaching and learning is always a work in progress.

**Work can be exhibited.** If students design their own escape rooms, then exhibition of students' efforts will be built-in. This is because students share what they have created for participants to experience. As mentioned, these participants can be fellow classmates, other students in the school, or even the broader school community (e.g., parents, families, or anyone who is invited to attend).

Beyond inviting people to experience the escape challenge, it is also a good idea to document, display, and maintain an exhibition of students' work. Doing so can ensure that the creative contribution of students' efforts can continue to be made long after the students have completed the work.

If you were to use this form of creative curriculum in your classroom, you might create a page on your classroom website that houses each of the escape challenges your current, past, and future students have designed. You can include a small thumbnail image of the escape room, a brief description, a list of materials, photos and descriptions of puzzles, a video walk through, and even (anonymous) student reflections of what they learned from engaging in the process.

You can then share this link with future students, colleagues, and anyone who is interested in this form of creative curriculum. Models and examples of creative work can serve as a powerful (and sometimes necessary) support for inspiring the creative work of others (Root-Bernstein & Root-Bernstein, 2006).

**Focus on process.** Creative curricular experiences often result in students actually *creating* something. And, in the case of the creative escape challenge, students will be designing and producing a tangible experience. A potential pitfall with creative curricula is that too much focus can be placed on a product (recall the product hazard discussed in chapter 2).

Given that creative curricula are part of students' learning experience, the focus should be placed on what they learned from the process. They will still use the products they produced as the context for their reflections (e.g., the puzzles they made, the escape challenge experience they designed), but the focus will be on the process they went through to produce their escape challenges and what they learned from that process.

In this way, even if things do not turn out as expected (e.g., a puzzle they designed didn't work, the puzzles were too easy or too difficult) or they ran into major setbacks (e.g., they didn't finish some of design elements, they forgot a major piece, they didn't work well together), they still have an opportunity to discuss what they have learned from the process, what they learned about creativity, and what they learned about themselves.

**Informs instruction.** When using creative curricular experiences, like having students design an escape room, you'll want to think about how you can ensure that you are gathering information that can help guide your instructional decisions and provide timely supports to students. There are a couple of easy ways to collect this kind of information.

Making observations on a simple note-pad can be a very effective way to jot down common issues or confusions you are noticing as you check in with students. You might realize that several students are struggling with how to come up with a theme for their escape challenge or that the puzzles they are designing are too easy or too complex.

Depending on the situation, you might intervene by stopping work and providing more clarification or examples or wait until the next class meeting to address issues that require more intensive support. Another effective way of gathering information that can help you guide your instruction is to use formative assessments, such as exit tickets (Wiliam, 2011).

At the end of each class session, you can have students or teams of students provide you with a quick update on any information that you would find helpful (e.g., their progress, how well their teams are working together, and any other questions or comments they have).

Finally, having students reflect on their experience with this type of creative curricular experience can provide helpful information for whether and how you might alter or use it with future students. Asking your students simple questions can go a long way in helping you gather information for subsequent planning and use of creative curricular experience in your classroom.

Examples include:

- *What suggestions would you have for next year's students when they design their escape rooms?*
- *What do you wish you knew at the beginning that you know now?*
- *What would have helped improve or make this an even better experience?*
- *What is your biggest takeway from this experience?*
- *What could I have done to better support you in this process?*

## SUMMARIZING ACTION PRINCIPLE

*If* you want to maximize the potential of using creative curricula in your classroom, *then* you need to ensure those curricular experiences provide students with structured and supportive learning opportunities to take creative action, learn from those actions, and make a creative contribution to others.

There is a seemingly endless variety of teaching tools, technologies, and techniques available. And each year more options are added. Trying to keep up with all these options can be overwhelming and leave you feeling like you are always falling behind in the kinds of creative learning experiences you could or should be providing for your students. Indeed, each new tool seems to promise a more creative approach for teaching and learning.

As has been discussed, there are no magic bullets when it comes to creativity. The quest for "instant creativity" has long been recognized as misguided (Barron 1969). Indeed, creative curricular experiences are less about *what* particular technology or technique you use. Rather, creative curricular experiences are about *how* you use and design experiences for students.

The goal of this chapter was to highlight some key considerations for the *how* of creative curricula, rather than the *what*. Taking the beautiful risk of using creative curriculum in your teaching ultimately has the goal of using academic content as a vehicle for creative learning. It is less about finding something radically new and more about trying out different ways of opening up your existing curricular goals and practices.

## NOTE

1. The observational matrix is available at https://dschool.stanford.edu/s/Puzzle-Bus-Observation-Matrix.pdf.

# Epilogue

## *The Beautiful Risk*
## *of Starting Today and Every Day*

The creative act aims at total renewal of the world.

—Jean-Paul Sartre

It's your turn. Given all the possibilities for how you can encourage and take beautiful risks in teaching and learning, how might you start? The answer is somewhat simple. Commit to asking yourself: *How might I take or encourage just one beautiful risk in my teaching or life today?*

Throughout this book you have been introduced to several beautiful risks that you and your students can take to establish a classroom supportive of creative teaching and learning. Regardless of where you start, the most important thing is to commit today and every day to beautiful risk taking. No matter how big or small the beautiful risk, make it a habit to encourage and take them.

Lead by example. Recognize and applaud those who have taken beautiful risks themselves. Step into the uncertainty. Take action. Learn from setbacks. Keep trying. And persist in striving to make and support the creative contributions you and your students are capable of making.

# References

Amabile, T. M. (1996). *Creativity in context: Update to the social psychology of creativity.* Boulder, CO: Westview.

Argyris, C., & Schön, D. A. (1974). *Theory in practice: Increasing professional effectiveness.* San Francisco: Jossey-Bass.

Baer, J. (2015). *Domain specificity of creativity.* San Diego, CA: Academic Press.

Baer, J., & McKool, S. (2009). Assessing creativity using the consensual assessment technique. In G. Christopher & S. Schreiner (Eds.), *Handbook of research on assessment technologies, methods, and applications in higher education* (pp. 65–77). Hershey, PA: Information Science Publishing.

Bandura, A. (1997). *Self-efficacy: The exercise of control.* New York: Freeman.

Bandura, A. (2006). Guide for constructing self-efficacy scales. In F. Pajares & T. Urdan (Eds.), *Self-efficacy beliefs of adolescents* (pp. 307–337). Greenwich, CT: Information Age.

Barker, R. G., & Wright, H. F. (1971). *Midwest and its children.* Hamden, CT: Archon.

Barron, F. (1969). Creative person and creative process. New York: Holt, Rinehart, & Winston.

Beghetto, R. A. (2010). Creativity in the classroom. In J. C. Kaufman & R. J. Sternberg (Eds.), *Handbook of Creativity.* New York: Cambridge University Press.

Beghetto, R. A. (2013). *Killing ideas softly? The promise and perils of creativity in the classroom.* Charlotte, NC: Information Age.

Beghetto, R. A. (2014). Creative mortification: An initial exploration. *Psychology of Aesthetics, Creativity, and the Arts, 8,* 266–276.

Beghetto, R. A. (2016a). *Big wins, Small steps: How to lead for and with creativity.* Thousand Oaks, CA: Corwin Press.

Beghetto, R. A. (2016b). Creative learning: A fresh look. *Journal of Cognitive Education and Psychology, 15,* 6–23.

Beghetto, R. A. (2016c). Creative openings in the social interactions of teaching. *Creativity: Theories—Research—Applications, 3,* 261–273.

Beghetto, R. A. (2017a). Creativity and conformity. In J. A. Plucker (Ed.), *Creativity and innovation: Current understandings and debates*. Waco, TX: Prufrock.

Beghetto, R. A. (2017b). Lesson unplanning: Toward transforming routine problems into non-routine problems. *ZDM—The International Journal on Mathematics Education*. DOI 10.1007/s11858-017-0885-1.

Beghetto, R. A. (2018). *What if? Unleashing the power of complex challenges in teaching and learning*. Alexandria, VA: ASCD.

Beghetto, R. A., & Breslow, J. Z. (2017). Creativity strategies. In K. Peppler (Ed.), *SAGE encyclopedia of out-of-school learning*. Thousand Oaks, CA: Sage.

Beghetto, R. A., & Dilley, A. E. (2016). Creative aspirations or pipe dreams? Toward understanding creative mortification in children and adolescents. *New Directions for Child and Adolescent Development, 151*, 85–95.

Beghetto, R. A., & Karwowski, M. (2017). Toward untangling creative self-beliefs. In M. Karwowski & J. C. Kaufman (Eds.), *The creative self* (pp. 3–22). San Diego, CA: Academic Press.

Beghetto, R. A., & Kaufman, J. C. (2007). Toward a broader conception of creativity: A case for mini-c creativity. *Psychology of Aesthetics, Creativity, and the Arts, 1*, 73–79.

Beghetto, R. A., Kaufman, J. C., & Baer, J. (2015). *Teaching for creativity in the common core*. New York: Teachers College Press.

Biro, D., & Fine, J. (Directors). (2006). *Herbie Hancock: Possibilities*. New York: Magnolia Pictures.

Black, P., & Wiliam, D. (1998). Inside the black box: Raising standards through classroom assessment. *Phi Delta Kappan, 80*, 139–148.

Breakwell, G. M. (2014). *The psychology of risk* (2nd ed.). Cambridge, UK: Cambridge University Press.

Byrnes, J. P. (2011). *The nature and development of decision-making: A self-regulation model*. New York: Psychology Press.

Cai, J., Ding, M., & Wang, T. (2014). How do exemplary Chinese and U.S. mathematics teachers view instructional coherence? *Educational studies in mathematics: An international journal, 85*, 265–280.

Callahan, C., Saye, J., & Brush, T. (2014). Social studies teachers' interactions with second generation web-based educative curriculum. *The Journal of Social Studies Research, 38*, 129–141.

Cazden, C. B. (2001). *Classroom discourse: The language of teaching and learning* (2nd ed.). Portsmouth, NH: Heinemann.

Chen, B. B. (2016). The creative self-concept as a mediator between openness to experience and creative behaviour. *Creativity: Theories–Research–Applications, 3*, 408–417.

Clark, C. (1983). Research on teacher planning: An inventory of the knowledge base. *DOCUMENT RESUME ED 237 455-SP 022 600, 400*, 4.

Clark, C. M., & Yinger, R. J. (1977). Research on teacher thinking. *Curriculum Inquiry, 7*, 279–304.

Cohen, L. M. (1989). A continuum of adaptive creative behaviors. *Creativity Research Journal, 2*, 169–183.

Corazza, G. E. (2016). Potential originality and effectiveness: The dynamic definition of creativity. *Creativity Research Journal, 28,* 258–267.

Cropley, D. H., Cropley, A. J., Kaufman, J. C., & Runco, M. A. (Eds.). (2010). *The darkside of creativity.* New York: Cambridge University Press.

Darwin, F. (Ed.). (1888). *The life and letters of Charles Darwin.* (Vol 1.). London: John Murray.

DeMunn, N. W., & Snow, F. B. (Eds.). (1865). Discouraging attempts to sing. *The Rhode Island Schoolmaster, 11,* 88–89.

Diedrich, J., Jauk, E., Silvia, P. J., Gredlein, J. M., Neubauer, A. C., & Benedek, M. (2017). Assessment of real-life creativity: The Inventory of Creative Activities and Achievements (ICAA). *Psychology of Aesthetics, Creativity, and the Arts.* http://dx.doi.org/10.1037/aca0000137.

Doyle, W. (2006). Ecological approaches to classroom management. In C. M. Evertson & C. S. Weinstein (Eds.), *Handbook of classroom management: Research, practice, and contemporary issues* (pp. 97–125). Mahwah, NJ: Lawrence Erlbaum Associates.

Dweck, C. S. (2006). *Mindset: The new psychology of success.* New York: Random House.

Eberle, B. (1996). *SCAMPER: Games for imagination development.* Waco, TX: Prufrock Press.

Eysenck, M. W., & Keane, M. T. (2013). *Cognitive psychology: A student's handbook.* New York: Psychology Press.

Feist, G. J. (1998). A meta-analysis of personality in scientific and artistic creativity. *Personality and Social Psychology Review, 2,* 290–309.

Galluzzo, G. R., & Kacer, B. A. (1991). The best and worst of high school student teaching. Paper presented at the annual meeting of the American Educational Research Association, Chicago, IL.

Gawande, A. (2009). *The checklist manifesto: How to get things right.* New York: Metropolitan Books.

Glăveanu, V. P. (2011). Is the lightbulb still on? Social representations of creativity in a Western context. *The International Journal of Creativity & Problem Solving, 21,* 53–72.

Glăveanu, V., & Beghetto, R. A. (2016). The difference that makes a creative difference. In R. A. Beghetto & B. Sriraman (Eds.), *Creative contradictions in education: Cross-disciplinary paradoxes and perspectives.* Switzerland: Springer.

Grant, A., & Coyle, D. (2018). The process of building trust works in the opposite way that you think it does. Retrieved from https://work.qz.com/1241911/daniel-coyle-author-of-the-the-culture-code-says-building-trust-works-in-the-opposite-way-you-think-it-does/?mc_cid=015ae0d31b&mc_eid=427e2dccd0.

Greene, M. (1995). *Releasing the imagination: Essays on education, the arts, and social change.* San Francisco, CA: Jossey-Bass.

Heinrich, C. (2000). *Monet.* Cologne, Germany: Taschen.

Hennessey, B. A. (2017). Intrinsic motivation and creativity in the classroom: Have we come full circle? In R. A. Beghetto & J. C. Kaufman (Eds.), *Nurturing creativity in the classroom* (2nd ed.). New York: Cambridge University Press.

Henry, C. B. (2017). *Miles Davis: A research and information guide.* New York: Routledge.

Isaksen, S. G., & Treffinger, D. J. (2004). Celebrating 50 years of reflective practice: Versions of creative problem solving. *Journal of Creative Behavior, 38*, 75–101.

Jaffe, S. (2014). Massachusetts teachers aim to knock down "data walls." Retrieved from http://inthesetimes.com/working/entry/16276/massachusetts_teachers_ knock_down_data_walls.

Jang, H., Reeve, J., & Deci, E. L. (2010). Engaging students in learning activities: It is not autonomy support or structure but autonomy support and structure. *Journal of educational psychology, 102*, 588–600.

Jurow, A. S., & Creighton, L. (2005). Improvisational science discourse: Teaching science in two K-1 classrooms. *Linguistics and Education, 16*, 275–297.

Karwowski, M. (2014). Creative mindsets: Measurement, correlates, consequences. *Psychology of Aesthetics, Creativity, and the Arts, 8*, 62–70.

Karwowski, M., & Beghetto, R. A. (in press). Creative behavior as agentic action. *Psychology of Aesthetics, Creativity, and the Arts.* http://dx.doi.org/10.1037/ aca0000190.

Karwowski, M., Lebuda, I., & Beghetto, R. A. (2018). Creative self-beliefs. In J. C. Kaufman & R. J. Sternberg (Eds.), *Cambridge Handbook of Creativity.* New York: Cambridge University Press.

Karwowski, M., Lebuda, I., Wisniewska, E., & Gralewski, J. (2013). Big five personality traits as the predictors of creative self-efficacy and creative personal identity: Does gender matter? *The Journal of Creative Behavior, 47*, 215–232.

Kaufman, J. C. (2016). Creativity 101 (2nd ed.). New York: Springer.

Kaufman, J. C., & Beghetto, R. A. (2009). Beyond big and little: The four C model of creativity. *Review of General Psychology, 13*, 1–12.

Kaufman, J. C., & Beghetto, R. A. (2013). In praise of Clark Kent: Creative metacognition and the importance of teaching kids when (not) to be creative. *Roeper Review, 35*, 155–165.

Kennedy, M. (2005). *Inside teaching: How classroom life undermines reform.* Cambridge, MA: Harvard University Press.

Kirschner, P. A., & van Merriënboer, J. J. (2013). Do learners really know best? Urban legends in education. *Educational psychologist, 48*(3), 169–183.

Kruger, J., & Dunning, D. (1999). Unskilled and unaware of it: how difficulties in recognizing one's own incompetence lead to inflated self-assessments. *Journal of Personality and Social Psychology, 77*, 1121–1134.

Lampert, M., Rittenhouse, P., & Crumbaugh, C. (1996). Agreeing to disagree: Developing sociable mathematical discourse. In D. R. Olson & N. Torrance (Eds.), *The handbook of education and human development: New models of learning, teaching, and schooling* (pp. 731–764). Cambridge, MA: Blackwell.

Leikin, R., & Kawass, S. (2005). Planning teaching an unfamiliar mathematics problem: The role of teachers' experience in solving the problem and watching pupils solving it. *The Journal of Mathematical Behavior, 24*(3–4), 253–274.

Mack, A., & Rock, I. (1998). *Inattentional blindness.* Cambridge, MA: MIT press.

McKay, J., & Kember, D. (1997). Spoon feeding leads to regurgitation: A better diet can result in more digestible learning outcomes. *Higher Education Research & Development, 16*(1), 55–67.

Mehan, H. (1979). *Learning lessons: Social organization in the classroom.* Cambridge, MA: Harvard University Press.

Midgley, C. (Ed.). (2002). *Goals, goal structures, and patterns of adaptive learning.* Mahwah, NJ: Elrbaum.

Mumford, M. D., Blair, C., Dailey, L., Leritz, L. E., & Osburn, H. K. (2006). Errors in creative thought? Cognitive biases in a complex processing activity. *The Journal of Creative Behavior, 40*, 75–109.

Nickerson, R. S. (1999). Enhancing creativity. In R. J. Sternberg (Ed.), *Handbook of human creativity.* New York: Cambridge University Press.

Orenstein, P. (2011). How to unleash your creativity. Retrieved from http://www.oprah.com/spirit/How-to-Unleash-Your-Creativity.

Plucker, J. A., Beghetto, R. A., & Dow, G. T. (2004). Why isn't creativity more important to educational psychologists? Potential, pitfalls, and future directions in creativity research. *Educational Psychologist, 39*, 83–97.

Pretz, J. E., & Nelson, D. (2017). Creativity is influenced by domain, creative self-efficacy, mindset, self-efficacy, and self-esteem. In M. Karwowski & J. C. Kaufman (Eds.), *The creative self: Effects of self-efficacy, mindset and identity* (pp. 155–170). San Diego, CA: Academic Press.

Renzulli, J. (2016). Developing creativity across all areas of the curriculum. In R. A. Beghetto & J. C. Kaufman, (2016). (Eds.), *Nurturing creativity in the classroom,* 2nd ed. (pp. 265–286). New York: Cambridge University Press.

Roberts, L., Dutton, J., Spreitzer, G., Heaphy, E., & Quinn, R. (2005). Composing the reflected best self portrait: Building pathways for becoming extraordinary in work organizations. *Academy of Management Review, 30*, 712–736.

Roberts, L., Spreitzer, G., Dutton, J., Quinn, R., Heaphy, E., & Barker, B. (2005). How to play to your strengths. *Harvard Business Review, 83*, 75–80.

Runco, M. A. (1996). Personal creativity: Definition and developmental issues. *New Directions in Child Development, 72*, 3–30.

Runco, M. A. (2005). Motivation, competence, and creativity. In A. Elliott & C. Dweck (Eds.), *Handbook of achievement motivation and competence* (pp. 609–623). New York: Guilford.

Runco, M. A., & Charles, R. E. (1993). Judgments of originality and appropriateness as predictors of creativity. *Personality and Individual Differences, 15*, 537–546.

Runco, M., & Jaeger, G.J. (2012). The standard definition of creativity. Creativity Research Journal, 21, 92–96.

Sawyer, R. K. (2004). Improvised lessons: Collaborative discussion in the constructivist classroom. *Teaching Education, 15*, 189–201.

Sawyer, R. K. (2016). Learning for creativity. In R. A. Beghetto & J. C. Kaufman (Eds.), *Nurturing creativity in the classroom,* 2nd ed. (pp. 265–286). New York: Cambridge University Press.

Scott, G., Leritz, L. E., & Mumford, M. D. (2004). The effectiveness of creativity training: A quantitative review. *Creativity Research Journal, 16*, 361–388.

Scott, M. M. (2005). A powerful theory and a paradox: Ecological psychologists after Barker. *Environment and Behavior, 37*(3), 295–329.

Sefton-Green, J. (2011). Judgement, authority, and legitimacy: Evaluating creative learning. In J. Sefton-Green, P. Thomson, K. Jones, & L. Bresler (Eds.), *The Routledge international handbook of creative learning* (pp. 311–319). London: Routledge.

Simonton, D. K. (2017). Defining creativity: Don't we also need to define what is *not* creative? *Journal of Creative Behavior, 51*, 281–284.

Skinner, E. A., & Belmont, M. J. (1993). Motivation in the classroom: Reciprocal effects of teacher behavior and student engagement across the school year. *Journal of educational psychology, 85*, 571–581.

Smith, J. K., & Smith, L. F. (2017). The 1.5 criterion model of creativity: Where less is more, more or less. *Journal of Creative Behavior, 51*, 281–284.

Stein, M. I. (1953). Creativity and culture. *The Journal of Psychology, 36*, 311–322.

Stein, M. I. (1987). Creativity research at the crossroads: A 1985 perspective. *Frontiers of creativity research: Beyond the basics* (pp. 417–427). Buffalo, NY: Bearly.

Stiggins, R. J. (2002). Assessment crisis: The absence of assessment for learning. *Phi Delta Kappan, 83*, 758–765.

Stokes, P. D. (2006). *Creativity from constraints: The psychology of breakthrough.* New York, NY: Springer Publishing Company.

Stokes, P. D. (2010). Using constraints to develop creativity in the classroom. In R. A. Beghetto & J. C. Kaufman (Eds)., *Nurturing creativity in the classroom* (pp. 88–112). Cambridge, UK: Cambridge University Press.

Troxler, D. (1804). On the disappearance of given objects from our visual field. In K. Himly & J. A. Schmidt (Eds.), Ophthalmologisches Bibliothek (pp. 51–53). Jena, Germany: Fromman.

Wiemker, M., Elumir, E., & Clare, A. (2015). Escape Room Games. Retrieved from https://thecodex.ca/wp-content/uploads/2016/08/00511Wiemker-et-al-Paper-Escape-Room-Games.pdf.

Wiliam, D. (2011). *Embedded formative assessment*. Bloomington, IN: Solution Tree Press.

Whiteley, G. (Director). (2015). *Most likely to succeed*. One Potato Productions.

# About the Author

**Dr. Ronald A. Beghetto** is an internationally recognized expert on creativity in educational settings. He serves as professor of educational psychology in the Neag School of Education and director of the Innovation House at the University of Connecticut. He is also editor-in-chief for the *Journal of Creative Behavior*, Fellow of the American Psychological Association (Div. 10, APA), and a creativity advisor for the Lego Foundation.

Dr. Beghetto has published eight books and over 100 articles and scholarly book chapters on creative and innovative approaches to teaching, learning, and leadership in schools and classrooms. He speaks and provides workshops around the world on issues related to helping teachers and instructional leaders develop new and transformative possibilities for classroom teaching, learning, and leadership in K-12 and higher education settings.